Arizona Trails & Tales

True Adventures in Arizona's Old West

by
Charles D. Lauer

Front cover: *The Arrest Of Nock-ay-del-klinne* by Francis Beaugureau

Back cover: (Top) *Remains of King Woolsey's ranchhouse.* (Below and left to right) *Jeremiah (Jere) Fryer, Chase Creek Street in Clifton (1910), Jack Swilling, Classic Concord Stagecoach, Pauline Cushman* and *Geronimo (Apache Indian Chief)*

Other Books by Charles D. Lauer:

> *Arrows, Bullets and Saddle Sores*
>
> *Old West Adventures in Arizona*
>
> *Tales of Arizona Territory*

Library of Congress Cataloging-in-Publication Data

Lauer, Charles D., 1919-
    Arizona trails & tales: true adventures in Arizona's Old West / by Charles D. Lauer.
        p. cm.
    Includes bibliographical references (p.).
    Includes Index
    ISBN 1-885590-86-5 (alk. paper)
    1. Arizona--History--Anecdotes. 2. Arizona--History, Local--Anecdotes. 3. Frontier and pioneer life--Arizona--Anecdotes. 4. Arizona--Biography--Anecdotes. I. Title: Arizona trails and tales. II. Title.
F811.6 .L377 2000
979.1--dc21

000-52074

3rd printing © 2007

Printed in the United States of America

Golden West Publishers, Inc.
4113 N. Longview Ave.
Phoenix, AZ 85014, USA
(800) 658-5830

Visit our website: http://www.goldenwestpublishers.com

Dedication

To the memory of my parents:
Charles A. Lauer of Fredonia, Kansas,
and Cevilia Lingard Lauer of Albion, Iowa

Acknowledgment

Most of the material in this volume came from the files of the Arizona Historical Society in Tucson, The Arizona Historical Foundation and Arizona Collection in the Hayden Library, Arizona State University in Tempe, the Sharlot Hall Museum Research Library in Prescott, the Arizona Capitol Archives, and the Casa Grande Valley Historical Society.

Arizona Historical Society, Tucson: Biographical files of Charles F. Bennett, Charles J. Eastman, Andrew J. Doran, Joseph W. Wham. Reminiscences of A. F. Banta, Will C. Barnes, Charles F. Bennett, Charles M. Clark, Charles T. Connell, Alice F. Curnow, Andrew W. Doran, Charles J. Eastman, M. M. Elders, Arthur H. Elliott, James B. Glover, Anton Mazzanovich, Mike M. Rice, I. E. Solomon, Perry Wildman. *Sheriff Magazine,* January and February, 1949, issues, ephemeral files Crimes and Criminals, Wham Paymaster Robbery. Microfilmed newspaper files. Pictures, clippings, and maps from library's files.

Arizona Historical Foundation, Tempe: J. W. Evans biography, microfilmed newspaper files.

Sharlot Hall Museum Research Library, Prescott: Ephemeral files Stagecoach Lines, Stagecoach Stations, microfilmed newspaper files.

University of Arizona Library: *Cosmopolitan Magazine,* October, 1896, issue.

National Archives, Laguna Niguel, Calif.: Partial transcript of the Wham Army Paymaster Robbery trial.

Arizona Archives, Capitol Building, Phoenix: Cibicu Creek fight in Arizona, H. B. Wharfield, Col., USAF Ret., Sketch of Cibicu Battleground.

Casa Grande Valley Historical Society: Anonymous monograph, pictures and sketches.

Maps, sketches and pictures not otherwise credited are by the author or from the author's collection.

Contents

Preface

This book consists of stories of true events and about forgotten places in Arizona, from its Old West history. The history is so recent that it is still alive and vibrant and fascinating. New arrivals in modern Arizona are surprised to find how close to the surface the Old West is—that just off an interstate freeway a few feet the domain of the lizard, the rattlesnake and kit fox may still be untouched, or that some back country dirt road may end up at the ruins of some boom-and-bust ghost town.

One of the difficulties found by researchers into Arizona history is the variance in the accounts given about the same event by different people or by newspapers that reported it. One case is the career of U. S. Deputy Marshal Joe Evans. While he was still an agent for a stage line, he lost an arm as the result of a gunfight with a drunken stage driver. This was duly reported in the local newspaper, the *Arizona Miner* of Prescott, preserved on microfilm. It was also reported years later by one of Arizona's most eminent pioneers, Charles M. Clark, who no doubt knew Joe Evans personally and heard from Evans himself the story of the gunfight. The newspaper reported that it was Evans' left arm that had to be amputated; Clark states several times that Evans lost his right arm. Which to believe in the absence of any pictures of Evans? The account in this book says that Evans lost his left arm, since the newspaper story written at the time of the amputation may well have been more accurate than a report written forty years later.

There are also three stories of the makeup of a posse that appeared with Evans in Casa Grande when he arrived there to serve a writ of habeas corpus. One was written later by Sheriff A. J. Doran who was out of town when Evans arrived, another was written by eminent historian James Barney, who was not present at the time the incident occurred. The version given credence in this book is that by Mike M. Rice, who as a deputy sheriff was present and an eye-witness to the events.

At one time an amusing story, absolutely without basis in fact, was told, that Mickey Free, an Apache scout mentioned in this book, was half-Apache and half-Irish and had red hair. However, it has been established without question that his father was an Apache warrior and his mother a Mexican orphan girl. Since both races have nothing but coal-black hair, it is genetically impossible for their offspring to have red hair. Pictures of him are the ultimate proof. The author has found that eye-witness accounts are the most reliable, followed closely by newspaper stories and official reports, third party accounts should be verified if possible, and tales by well-meaning old-timers of today should be researched again.

Another subject that should be touched on is racial and ethnic relations. On the frontier they were a constant source of friction. Generally, the Americans, Mexicans and Indians as factions were each adverse to the other two and did not hesitate to express their aversions in racial epithets and violence. Even Europeans were polarized into ethnic groups, and brawls between Irish, Welsh, Italians, Poles, English, Slavs and other societies ruined more than one saloon. The true writer of historical events does not take sides or gloss over these happenings, but simply writes the truth as well as it can be discovered. Readers should be aware that historical reports of such racial and ethnic differences are just "telling it like it was."

One of the most intriguing things about Arizona history is that it is still possible today to visit the scenes of past events, see them as they are, and recall historical experiences at the spots they actually occurred. The author has attempted to provide maps, drawings and verbal descriptions of locations found in the text, so that readers so inclined may visit them. Many can now be reached only with difficulty over roads long abandoned, with the aid of a pick-up truck or four-wheel drive vehicle. This advice is included in the text. For those who undertake such a venture, a never-to-be-forgotten experience may be in store.

Most of the material in this book came from the Arizona Historical Society in Tucson, the Arizona Historical Foundation in the Hayden Library at Arizona State University in Tempe, the research library at Sharlot Hall Museum in Prescott, and the Casa Grande Valley Historical Society in Casa Grande. The author wishes to acknowledge his debt to them, and to thank the staffs of those institutions and any others that were consulted.

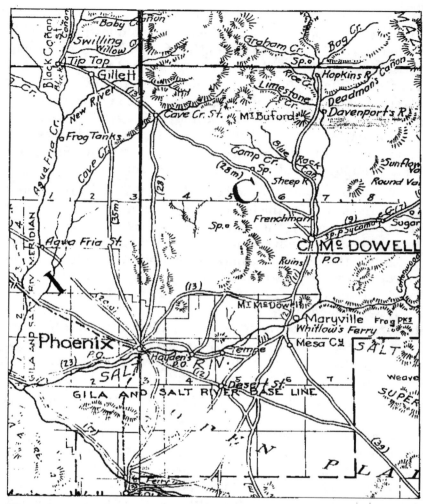

Note erroneous location of Gillett on map. Gillett actually stood where map shows Tiptop location. Tiptop's actual location was eight miles farther west.

BLACK CANYON STAGECOACH TRAIL, PHOENIX to CANON

from 1879 military map of Arizona

Chapter 1

The Black Canyon Stagecoach Trail

As the evening began to gather around the 'down' stage-coach, going down the Black Canyon trail from Prescott to Phoenix, Arizona Territory, Capt. C. G. Gordon began to worry. The town of Gillett was not far away now, and the trail approaching it from either north or south was notorious as the favorite haunt of the highwaymen who robbed the coaches so regularly that even Wells-Fargo Express Co. would eventually no longer accept shipments over it. The stagecoach had left Prescott at two in the afternoon, and it was August 26, 1882. Gordon, en route to his cavalry post at Camp Price, nervously commented to his fellow passengers that if they had any money with them, they had better stuff it into their boots, as they were liable to be held up at any time. The other passengers were Dr. Lord and I. E. Solomon, a prominent merchant from a town named for him, Solomonville, near Fort Grant.

Solomon's reply was that the captain had better hide his own money, too, as he probably had more on him than Solomon, who could afford to lose what little cash he had. In Prescott that morning, Solomon had cashed a check for $25 for expenses at C. P. Head & Co., though he also had with him two government checks, for $1,000 and $960, payment for supplies furnished to Fort Whipple near Prescott. Finally, Gordon left his seat inside the coach and climbed up on the outside seat beside the driver. The long Arizona summer day was over and darkness was closing in.

About two miles from Gillett, two masked men, one armed with a six-shooter and the other with a sawed-off shotgun, suddenly appeared beside the coach and ordered the driver to halt. One pointed a gun at Solomon and told him to get out. Solomon lost no time in obeying the order, nor did Dr. Lord or the captain who was told to get down into the road. At the command "Throw up your hands!" they also lost no time. The

Classic Concord Stagecoach such as used on the Black Canyon route. Passengers often rode on top. Wells-Fargo Express box was in the boot under the driver's feet. (Arizona Historical Society)

bandit with the shotgun presided over the proceedings, while his partner went through the victims' pockets. Solomon had an expensive gold watch that was attached with a silk cord. The robber started to untie the cord, but Solomon asked him to just cut the cord, which was done. Solomon's watch was taken, and so were those of Dr. Lord and Capt. Gordon. The captain's pockets yielded about $365 to the bandits, Dr. Lord's $50, and Solomon's $63. The checks they were carrying were returned as they were useless to anyone else.

Then the bandits ordered the driver to throw the Wells-Fargo treasure box out into the road. They had considerable difficulty breaking it open, and took the contents though there appeared to be nothing of value. During all this time there had been considerable good-humored conversation between the robbers and the stage passengers, Solomon taking the occasion to compliment the robbers on the success of their enterprise in getting a substantial amount of cash and other booty without doing bodily harm to anyone.

Just then sounds were heard indicating that the 'up' stage,

going up the canyon from Phoenix to Prescott, was approaching, having shortly before left Gillett. The Phoenix-bound passengers were told to stand quietly along the road behind the stopped coach. When the oncoming stagecoach reached the scene, it was surprised and halted by the highwaymen, who ordered the passengers into the road and relieved them of their guns. There were six men in the coach, including three soldiers, a Dr. Ainsworth, and Dave Naegle, a U. S. Deputy Marshal who once had been town marshal at Tombstone. With hands in the air they were also robbed of their money and watches. The Wells-Fargo treasure box was also rifled. As it contained a three-day accumulation of express shipments, speculation was that the yield was substantial.

Solomon again spoke up, complimenting the bandits on their successful enterprise in stopping two stagecoaches and making a good haul without causing any bodily harm. The two holdup men seemed to appreciate his remarks, emboldening Solomon.

From the conversation, he had thought that one of the bandits knew him, and he asked that one if he would be good enough to give him back his watch, which he prized highly as an heirloom as it had been given to him by a relative. Without hesitation, the robber handed it back to him. Solomon thanked him; then Capt. Gordon asked them to return his watch also. Solomon remarked that Gordon was a friend of his, and said that the bandits had made such a good haul they could afford to give it back. Gordon's watch was given back to him. Then Dave Naegle spoke up. "Gentlemen," he said, "I hope you will also return my watch. I prize it very highly because it was given to me by prominent citizens of Tombstone after I had served that city as chief of police. Their names and mine are engraved on the watch. If you will return it, I will leave, or send, $100 to any place in Arizona for you and never try to make any trouble for you because of the watch." The robbers hesitated but one finally said, "Here, take your confounded watch," and he got it back without any instruction about where to send the money he had promised.

The Prescott-bound 'up' stage was then ordered to move on, and Solomon again thanked the bandits for their "liberality" in returning the watches. He asked if they would also return enough for his breakfast and for drinks for the passengers. One of the bandits produced a handful of silver, held it out, and told him to take what he needed. Saying, "Boys, you seem to be regular fellers," Solomon took $7 or $8. The driver was then told to proceed on the way to Gillett.

Word of the robbery did not reach Prescott until ten the next morning, when Sheriff Orme and a Wells-Fargo representative immediately left for the robbery scene though there was little hope of arresting the robbers after a twenty-four hour start. It was believed that they got $1,000 to $1,200 in loot. Though the state offered a reward of $600, the county $600 and Wells-Fargo $300 for the capture of the bandits, there is no account that they were ever identified or caught.

The account of this holdup was printed in the *Arizona Gazette* newspaper of Phoenix on August 26, 1882. Other details were related by Solomon in his reminiscences years later. The Black Canyon stagecoach trail was an important necessity in territorial Arizona, though it was a secondary route between Prescott, the territorial capital, and Phoenix and points south.

The main Prescott-Phoenix road ran through Wickenburg, west of the rugged Bradshaw Mountains. It had the advantage of having flat deserts to cross most of the way. Wickenburg was also the hub of traffic to points west, the Colorado River ports and the burgeoning state of California. But east of Wickenburg and the high, rugged crests of the Bradshaw Mountains, little mining camps and ranches were springing up. Travel between them was mostly random, over trails and an old military road.

Then in 1875 two prospectors discovered the rich silver lode that became the Tiptop Mine in the mountains above the Agua Fria River some forty miles north of Phoenix. The mine's milling town, Gillett, was quickly established on the banks of the Agua Fria, and a Prescott-Phoenix road through Tiptop and Gillett became an absolute necessity. The trails were strung together through a series of stations and towns, and the Black Canyon highway became a reality.

Northward from Phoenix the stations were at the gold diggin's at Cave Creek, at New River, then Tiptop and Gillett.

Tradition says this old building stands on the exact spot at New River that was once the location of the original stage station.

The trail followed along the Agua Fria River to Canon (today's Black Canyon City) and Bumble Bee, and ascended into the mountains to Cordes Ranch and Mayer. Then it was on to Bowers Ranch near today's Dewey, and to other stops, varying over the years, to Prescott. Stations came and went along the line as demand dictated. A Prescott newspaper, the *Journal-Miner,* on August 6, 1898, listed the stations as Cave Creek, New River, Canon, Bumble Bee, Richinbar, Cordes, Mayer, Big Bug, Chaparral, McCabe and Prescott. Today, it is the busy I-17 to Cordes Junction, then northwest on U. S. 69 to Prescott.

The Black Canyon road from Phoenix ran north along Cave Creek road pretty much on the same alignment it does today. Prospectors had been sifting placer gold on the banks of Cave Creek Wash and Blue Wash, and gold lodes were being worked in the nearby desert hills. By 1876, two years before Gillett was founded, the Phoenix Mine and others at Cave Creek were furnishing ore for a ten-stamp mill. Cattle and sheep men had moved in to take up ranches, so when the gold supply proved to be limited, ranching dominated life at Cave Creek.

General George Stoneman started a military road from Fort McDowell on the Verde River northeast of Phoenix toward Fort Whipple at Prescott. At Cave Creek he had a small rock fort and stage station built. Part of its walls still stand today, incorporated into the home of a family living there.

From Cave Creek the road wound through the desert to the bank of New River and the New River Stage Station. Tradition says it was on the spot the present road near the freeway crosses

New River in the shadow of Gavilan Peak, and the rock portion of a service station there are the remains of the stage station. Tradition also says it was run for a while by Darrel Duppa, one of the famed founders of Phoenix and friend of Arizona pioneer Jack Swilling residing in Gillett and Canon a short distance north.

There is only passing mention of the New River station in accounts of early Arizona, confirming that there was one. The *Arizona Sentinel* of Yuma said on August 22, 1875, that New River station keeper John White had been held up and robbed by Mexicans. September 25th that year the *Sentinel* said that, because the region was so infested with bandits and robbers, the station was closed, and hinted the route might be changed.

The Black Canyon stage trail continued up along the bank of New River for some distance, then turned west past Table Mesa into the Bradshaw Mountains to the mining camp at Tiptop. The prospectors who discovered the silver claim in 1875 sold it in 1877 to San Francisco investors for $85,000 and the mine was rapidly developed. The camp was a lively place, strewn along the canyon, with perhaps 250 residents most of whom were miners, but with some families and businessmen.

"Oh, how I wish that I owned a 'dab' in the Tiptop Mine," wailed a correspondent of the *Arizona Miner* in its October 11, 1878, issue. "The Tiptop town is no sardine of a place. The traveler entering the town by the stage road from Gillett passes first the residence of the demi-monde (ladies of shady reputation), then a whiskey mill, then another whiskey mill, then the butcher shop, passes Mr. Neff's residence and corral. . . Next in line is another gin mill, then another and another, passes 'Mexico,' the company's blacksmith shop, boarding house and office which are all good buildings. Next is the residence and shoe shop of Mr. Chas. Shultz and family, then the trail crosses the creek bed—no water—climbs a short grade and passes the courthouse and another gin mill, then Anders and Rowe's store. . . The last is Joe Mayer's restaurant, where a good table is presided over by Mrs. Mayer and awaits the hungered pilgrims who, when fed there, always have a 'hankering' to again partake of Joe's culinary productions."

The Tiptop camp was rather quiet compared with others, but had its rowdy moments. The *Miner* reported that on September 19th "James Short, a Catholic, and Hugh Ross, an Orangeman, got too much benzene in their noses and quarreled about religious beliefs, etc., which resulted in Ross trying to dissect his opponent with a large butcher knife. Ross was arrested and examined, defended by Judge Handy, and held to appear at the next term of court. Short's wound while quite painful was not serious, and he is now doing well. . . The camp is in great need of a deputy sheriff and constable."

The richness of the Tiptop ore started a rush to the district, and several other mines including the Black Jack, 76, Eldorado, and Brutus among them were located, but none ever approached the success of the Tiptop. The company had a mill shipped in and erected on the bank of the Agua Fria River, eight miles below the mine. "The Tiptop company has a large force of men opening a wagon road from the mill site to the mine," said the *Arizona Miner* on January 18, 1878. "It is the intention of the company to push the road on into the Bradshaw Mountains, where they will erect a sawmill and manufacture lumber to be used in building a large town adjacent to where they are putting up their mill."

The mill town, of course, became Gillett. It was named for the mine superintendent, Dan B. Gillett, by the citizenry at a mass meeting on January 22, 1878, said the *Miner* on February 1st. This town, rather than the Tiptop mining camp, became the favorite haunt of the denizens of the Black Canyon country. Besides the mill, it had all the usual ingredients of the wild-west town—stores, shops, businesses, respectable citizens, saloons, bawdy-houses, painted ladies, gamblers and gunmen. "Last night two men, Grindle and Calhoun, engaged in hard words over a game of cards in Levy's saloon," reported the *Miner's* correspondent in its March 6, 1878, issue. "Calhoun went out to the north side of the house and, taking deliberate aim, shot Grindle through the body, the ball penetrating vital parts. There can be no excuse tendered in palliation of this deed. Calhoun gave Grindle no opportunity to defend himself, but acted the dastardly and cowardly ruffian. . . Calhoun cleared the country after making the remark, 'Sam, we have a man for breakfast, but I swear I did not shoot him. Grindle cannot live. . .'"

The next station north of Gillett on the Black Canyon route was at Canon, the location of the Black Canyon City of today. Not much has been preserved of the station's early years, and though Jack Swilling had a ranch near there he never was the station keeper. As late as 1903 the station was still in operation, and was the scene of a double murder. It made headlines in the *Arizona Republican* of Phoenix on February 3, 1903, having taken place the day before. The station keeper then was Charlie Goddard, who with his brother Frank also ran a sheep-shearing operation there using a steam-powered device they had invented.

Some time previously, two sheep shearers had gotten into a fight, which Goddard broke up by pistol-whipping one of the combatants. Vowing vengeance, the Mexican who was named Francisco Rentezia left the station. He enlisted the assistance of a friend, Hilario Hidalgo. They bought two used Colt .45s at a second-hand store in Prescott, and returned to Canon intending to kill Goddard and rob the station. They approached Goddard's dwelling on a Sunday evening just as the occupants were sitting down to dinner. These were Charles Goddard and his wife, Frank Goddard, teamster Frank Cox, and Milton Turnbull, an invalid miner. The Mexicans entered and demanded food, and Goddard, not recognizing them, told them they would have to wait until the family was finished eating.

At this Rentezia jerked his gun and shot Charles Goddard just below the heart. As he fell, another shot through the head of Frank Cox killed him instantly. The rest of the family dived under the table, and somehow the lamp was extinguished. Having no idea how many were dead or if any of the others had guns, the Mexicans fled without attempting the robbery. The survivors did not dare an attempt to move during the night, fearing more bullets, except for the wounded Goddard who dragged himself to a couch where he expired the next morning.

Sheriff Roberts took up the trail and traced the murderers to Naco, where he heard that the two men were working on a railroad just below the Mexican border. He persuaded some section hands to lure them back to the American side on some pretext, then promptly arrested them and returned them in shackles to Prescott. The trial was quick and justice was swift. On the morning of July 30, 1903, they were hanged in the courtyard of the jailhouse in Prescott.

Old building in ghost town of Bumble Bee. No buildings there now date from territorial days.

Northward from Canon the next station was Bumble Bee. It got its unusual name from nearby Bumble Bee Creek, where some prospectors looking for placer gold had been set upon by a swarm of the insects. The station keeper was W. W. Snyder who also had a ranch there. One harrowing trip on the Black Canyon route began with violence at Bumble Bee, reported by the *Phoenix Gazette* early in November, 1882. "When the coach arrived at Bumble Bee (the 'down' stage) Peter Conelly in charge of the stock turned loose with a pistol on Jim Wagner, the driver. Wagner secured his own pistol from the seat and returned the fire. Both men emptied their pistols, then it was discovered that Conelly had been shot in the leg and a horse wounded in the neck. It being dark accounts for the lightness of the casualties. An army surgeon was on board, and after waiting on the wounded man and stanching the flowing blood of the horse, the trip was resumed.

"At Gillett, however, a more serious affray occurred. Jim McClintock, the driver, and Joe Coulson, stage agent, were quarreling, the former being somewhat intoxicated. After getting off the box, McClintock wrapped the lines on the brake and got off for the purpose of whipping Coulson. The latter warned him not to approach, but paying no heed thereto McClintock advanced upon Coulson, who drew his pistol and fired—the muzzle of the weapon being pressed against McClintock's stomach. The ball passed through the body and on into the coach, narrowly missing one of the passengers. Coulson then fired another shot and the ball penetrated the body of his victim. Mr. McClintock was alive when the stage left, but it was not presumed that he could live many hours. It was a very sad trip and the passengers never before experienced anything as eventful and sanguinary."

Another hair-raising stagecoach ride down the mountainside between Bumble Bee and Canon was described in a clipping from an unidentified Phoenix newspaper on September 1, 1895. "Z. C. McCullough drives for J. B. Hocker on the Black Canyon line between this city and Prescott, . . the section of the line between Mayer and Canon. On this occasion there was but one passenger, John Q. White, the painter and paper-hanger, who got on at Bumble Bee. Just as they rounded the hilltop at Black Canyon Hill, about 10 o'clock at night, a man was noticed standing near the roadside.

"Halt! Halt!" yelled the would-be robber, but the wagon brake was screeching and the men did not pay particular attention until 'biz' came a rifle ball from the Winchester, cutting near their heads. The mules fairly flew, being frightened at the shot, and they did not stop running until they reached the foot of the steep hill. . . It was a daring ride over one of the roughest roads in Arizona, but the driver sat steady and steered the runaways around the complex curves and over steep grades while the lumbering stage jostled from side to side. The men every moment expected to be dashed on the rocks below, but the outfit held the trail though at full speed. Nothing more was seen of the robber. . ."

With the volume of traffic over the route after the establishment of Tiptop and Gillett making it a profitable run, a number of stage companies competed for the business. "The stage running from Prescott to Gillett, under management of Cusicks and Murphy, is quite an improvement over the old buckboard," observed the *Arizona Miner* of Prescott on March 6, 1878. "Mr. Murphy is an old stage man, having served at his profession in California, and we can safely guarantee through his hands the stage business between here and Tiptop being carried on properly."

Just over a week later, March 15th, the *Miner* reported that "Patterson, Caldwell & Levally (P. C. & Co.) have purchased the stage line that has hitherto run from Phoenix to Gillett, and will hereafter run through twice a week, from Prescott to Phoenix via Agua Fria, Big Bug, Cottonwood, Bumble Bee, Black Canyon, Gillett, Tiptop, Humbug, etc. The first coach left the Plaza Stables this morning with six passengers and a heavy load of private mail..." The article went on to gripe, repeated in several following issues, about the lack of mail service over the route. Until bids were sought and a contract awarded, mail had to be privately delivered or addressed to Phoenix or Prescott to be picked up.

Despite high expectations, P. C. & Co. went broke when a competing stage line underbid them for the mail contract. The owners of P. C. & Co. secretly gathered up their stock and equipment, and with their families tried to flee without anyone knowing—especially the creditors to whom several thousand dollars was due. When the flight was discovered, some of the creditors accompanied by a constable with a writ of attachment pursued the deadbeats and extracted a settlement.

Kerens and Griffith, the successful bidders for the mail contract, became the predominant stage company over the Black Canyon route and continued so for some years. R. C.

Ghost town of Bumble Bee, once a station on the Black Canyon route, in the Agua Fria River valley at the foot of the Bradshaw Mountains, as seen from the Sunset Point rest stop on I-17.

Kerens was a veteran stage coacher, once a partner in the stage line over the old Butterfield trail across southern Arizona, and Bill Griffith a capable manager. The *Miner* announced on January 22, 1880, that schedule time between Prescott and Phoenix of Kerens and Griffith's route would be 22 hours over the Black Canyon trail.

The Black Canyon route ascended from about a thousand feet in altitude at Phoenix to the mile-high altitude at Prescott (or the other way around) during its run. It began in the desert environment of cactus and greasewood, passed through the junipers and yuccas as the altitude increased, and ended in the pines and scrub oaks of the mountains. This meant changes in the weather, too, which could become drastic according to the season. It caused some dangerous, adventurous journeys with enough excitement to satisfy even the most daring.

One of these comes from the reminiscences of Will C. Barnes, distinguished Arizona pioneer, forest service employee, rancher, original writer of the famed *Arizona Place Names* reference book. Barnes did not identify the stage line involved in this tale, which began in Prescott.

"Six o'clock in the morning, dark and cold, a foot of snow on the ground," he began. "The huge Concord 'thorough brace' stage stood in front of the hotel at Prescott. The passengers were already climbing into its dark depths." They were two middle-aged nuns, Sisters of Charity dressed in their distinctive garb; William O. "Buckey" O'Neill, tall, dark and handsome politician and sheriff, who as a captain of the Rough Riders fell at San Juan Hill in the Spanish-American War; Price Behan, politician, ex-sheriff and father of Johnny Behan who was sheriff at Tombstone during the time Wyatt Earp was U. S. Marshal there; a young commercial traveler from San Francisco making his first visit to Arizona; and Barnes, then a range cattleman, together with the stage driver, a typical character of the old stage days.

The passengers stowed themselves inside the coach; every other space was crammed with U. S. mail sacks and express baggage. The first five or six miles were decidedly up-grade, and we will have reference to this hill again. Because of the weather, the driver was riding alone on the top, and at the crest of the grade he pulled up the team and clambered down from his high seat. It was daylight now, but the sun remained behind heavy clouds. "Muttering and cursing to himself," continued Barnes, "the driver stumbled through the deep snow to the heads of the leaders.

"O'Neill, watching him from the 'swing' seat of the coach, saw him pull a bottle from his overcoat pocket and take a long drink. A minute later the driver took his seat on top, gathered up his reins, threw the brake off, and gave a wild Apache yell. The team started off down the steep grade at a (brisk) trot, the coach swaying and rocking like a ship in heavy seas. It took but a few minutes to convince the men inside that the driver was drunk and would not or could not control his team. The heavy coach rocked and plunged along the rough road, skidded recklessly around curves, dropped into deep chuck holes covered by the snow. The driver with shrill yells even encouraged his team to increase their speed. The long lash curled over their backs as they tore down the rough grade. Drunk as he was, he wielded the whip with skill and accuracy.

"Inside the coach, the four men hastily decided on a plan of action. No time was to be lost. Prompt action alone could avert a bad accident." Behan, then a U. S. marshal, was on the inside left of the coach, the driver on the right side of his high, outside seat. Behan and O'Neill took their six-guns from their holsters and tucked them in their waist-bands, then Behan carefully opened the door, stood on the iron step, and reaching up, grasped the iron railing that ran round the top. O'Neill grasped Behan's other foot and gave a mighty shove upward, landing him on top of the stage directly back of the driver's seat. "Behan's left arm shot around that worthy's neck with a choking grip," continued Barnes, "while his right hand grabbed the reins from his clutching fingers. O'Neill, closely behind, pulled the Jehu from his seat and back onto the top of the stage.

"A clout on the side of the head from O'Neill's heavy six-shooter cured all desire on his part to fight back. A pair of handcuffs was snapped onto his wrists. Then as the team was stopped he was dragged unceremoniously to the ground, the big leather 'boot' behind the stage was unstrapped, and (still handcuffed) the driver was bundled into the boot, the cover pulled back into place and strapped down tightly. He made no further trouble. At noon, under Behan's expert driving, the stage reached the regular mail station (most probably Mayer) where always a new driver and team were furnished. The drunken driver, not yet sobered up, was turned over to the station keeper to be sent back to Prescott as a prisoner on the 'up' stage.

"No other driver being available, Behan agreed to drive the team down to the next (change) station, Gillett, some thirty-five miles south. The new team was a notable one in that region. Four fine mules, each as white as snow, perfectly matched as to size and gait—one of the most picturesque and unusual stage teams in all the far west. Young, lively, and full of pep they were 'just rarin' to go' when hitched up.

"The road now ran down the mountainside on a narrow shelf cut from the rocky walls. There was a mass of sharp curves and dangerous corners. As the stage dropped down into the lower altitudes it grew milder. The snow disappeared; deep mud took its place. Rain also began to fall in torrents. Progress was very slow. Darkness found the stage at the head of a long, narrow grade which ran for fifteen miles down the Black Canyon. The 'down' and 'up' stages usually met on this stretch. At every turn each driver stopped his team and 'stopped, looked, and listened.' Each peered into the (pitch-black) darkness, seeking the blinking lights of the other stage, a two-candle power lighting system that didn't shed its beams very far ahead.

"Each driver carried a long tin horn such as New England fishing smacks used in fogs. These were blown at regular intervals. A long blast was a warning, two short toots an acknowledgement. The system called for the 'up' stage to crawl into the first wide place in the road and wait for the 'down' stage. Crude as it was, the method worked fairly well for years. Occasionally a crash of thunder or some other noise would kill the sound of the horn, and the two stages met, perhaps at some point where passing was not possible. Then the 'up' team was unhitched and with two men at the tongue of the stage to guide it the heavy vehicle was rolled carefully back down the grade until a place was reached where it could be snuggled into a corner and allow the other to pass. . .

"Where the Black Canyon came out into the vast, open valley . . . the Agua Fria (had to be) forded to reach the stage station (at Gillett on the western side). The 'up' driver (had warned them) that this stream was running banks full and more. It was nearly midnight when the stage rolled out of the dark canyon onto the gravelly bank of the Agua Fria. The river was surely booming. O'Neill had taken turns driving and both men were soaked through and through and half frozen. The night air was keen and raw. Behan stopped the stage a few yards from the water's edge. Across the boiling, turbulent river they could see the lights of the station. They blinked and glowed in the dark like will-o'-the-wisps. Over there warmth and food awaited the weary, chilled travelers.

"The four men stood at the water's edge in the pelting rain studying the situation. Adventurers all, used to meeting difficult situations, they personally were willing to risk the crossing." But what about the two Sisters? They were huddled together in the dark coach shivering with cold. "O'Neill told them briefly of the situation of the danger in crossing under such conditions. They could wait for morning and hope for a drop in the stream's flow. . . Clear-eyed and unafraid, the elder of the two women spoke. 'Gentlemen,' she said, 'we are but two frail women. You men must decide. We leave it all to your good judgment. All of us are in the hands of our heavenly Father. He will surely answer our prayers for guidance and success.' Thus encouraged, the four men . . . made their plans for the crossing. Just below (it), the stream entered the canyon again. No one knew how deep the water was at the crossing. If deep enough to float the heavy stage, the whole affair might be swept down stream into the canyon and all be lost.

"Cold and numbed as they were, no one could possibly swim in such a swift current. It was agreed that Behan was to drive. A water bucket hung under the boot; O'Neill was to fill it with small stones to hasten the mules (by pelting them). The other two men, each with a Sister of Charity on his side, were to stand on the upstream side of the vehicle. There, holding tightly to the rail on top they were to lean far back and act as a sort of counter balance against the tremendous pressure of the swift stream against the side of the stage. They hoped the combined weight of the four would meet any tendency of the stage to overturn. In that event, it was agreed that each of the two men was to grab a Sister and do his best to get her safely to shore."

Behan and O'Neill climbed to the driver's seat. "All ready?" asked O'Neill, looking back at the four clinging to the coach's side. The two men looked at the two women. "All ready, gentlemen. The good God has us all in his protecting arms. He will not forsake us in the time of need."

"Behan loosed the brake and with a wild yell the mules lunged into the whirling water. O'Neill did his best by pelting the animals with rocks aimed with fine precision. Both men yelled like wild Indians. Behan lashed at them with his whip." As the leaders struck deep water and began to swim they were swept around with the current and downstream. The wheelers kept their feet a little while, then they too were forced to swim. Finally the huge stage itself floated free. The water was up to the knees of the four clinging to the side. Each was leaning back as far as possible to keep the stage from overturning. Behan, cool and collected, did his best to keep the team headed for the farther bank, and from becoming entangled in the harness and rigging.

As the coach swung around in the current, the downstream wheels struck a submerged rock. The coach began to rise slowly due to the tremendous pressure against the upper side. For one or two agonizing minutes it seemed that it would be turned over in the water and all would be lost. Just at this critical moment, when it seemed nothing could save them, the two little lead mules touched bottom with the points of their front feet. How those little fellows did claw and tear at the steep bank. Gradually they got the stage to move ahead. Then the long legged wheelers also touched bottom, and they clawed and dug as if realizing the need for every ounce of power.

Inch by inch the heavy stage began to move through the water toward the bank. Gradually it settled back to an even keel. It took the last rock in O'Neill's bucket plus much yelling and slashing of the whip to get up the steep bank and the whole outfit safely on solid land. "Three minutes later," Barnes wrote in conclusion, "Behan drove the team through the grove of

Remains of early station in Cave Creek are said to be part of this dwelling in that town.

cottonwoods to the station. The door flew open, a flood of light was in their eyes. Once inside, the two Sisters, wet and cold as they were, dropped to their knees, the men standing uncovered beside them in silent prayer."

Mike Rice, well-known and respected newspaperman and sometimes law officer on the Arizona frontier, left another exciting account of travel through the Black Canyon. Written many years after it occurred, it is filed at the Arizona Historical Society.

"It was raining slightly as we left Phoenix," begins Mike Rice's tale of adventure, "but increased in volume as we progressed toward the New River stage station, where we were held up at the crossing by the swift-flowing stream necessitating a lay-over until the torrent receded. I had arrived in Phoenix the day before Christmas, 1884, and there awaited the stage for Prescott going over the Black Canyon route. The driver's name I can't recall, but the list of passengers included Ed McGowan of vigilante fame, Billy Cuddy, late captain of the Salvation Army in Los Angeles, Georgia (Frankie) McClintock, sister of Col. James H. McClintock of Rough Rider fame, six

rookies who were to report to Fort Whipple at Prescott, and me."
Rice had been sent by L. C. Hughes, editor of the Tucson *Daily
Star* as the newspaper's correspondent to the session of the
Thirteenth Arizona Territorial Legislature, soon to convene at
Prescott, the capital.

"We were held up that night at New River by the torrent of
rain," continued Rice. "In the morning it cleared up somewhat
so we proceeded on our way to Tiptop. Here it continued to pour
down like a cloudburst, and an extra span of horses was
harnessed to the stagecoach to pull us through to the Bumble
Bee station. The road was in horrible condition; the wheels of
the coach became solid disks of adobe mud. The driver on
several occasions had to get down and dig the caked mud from
between the spokes. It commenced to snow and sleet at the foot
of the grade between Tiptop and the Bumble Bee station,
adding distress to the team and chagrin to the passengers. We
arrived at the station late that night and remained over until
morning. It continued to snow all night and by daylight the
ground was covered by a blanket of white a foot deep.

"Fortunately I carried a bundle of bedding in a canvas fly
tent, containing a 'colchon' (mattress) and two large mission
woolen blankets, and this proved to be a God-send to one of the
passengers, Miss McClintock. It saved her from serious injury
if not death, as we shall see. In the morning it was snowing
without any sign of let-up. Mrs. Snyder of the road house
assisted in wrapping Miss McClintock in my 'colchon' and
blankets, and made her as comfortable as possible in the
crowded coach. With six soldiers and McGowan inside she had
skimpy room for much comfort. Billy Cuddy and I rode outside
with the driver. I used my fly tent to cover Cuddy, the driver,
and myself.

"An additional span of horses was harnessed to the stagecoach at Bumble Bee making eight horses in the team. It took
us the whole day from Bumble Bee to Joe Mayer's station where
we made another overnight stay. Here we were royally entertained by the prince of station hosts, Joe Mayer, and here was
the start of future trouble. The soldiers and Cuddy secured
liquor; that boded no good for the passengers. It ceased snowing
during the night and the prospects looked favorable for a day

free from snow or rain. However, the snow was at least two feet deep at the level on the Bowers ranch when we arrived there.

"Here the driver was advised to lay over for the night to give the team a chance to rest and allow the passengers to stretch themselves, but he was obdurate. He said that 'he was already too damned long on the trip,' that he might be put on the carpet by the stage company, and his job was more to him than the inconvenience of his passengers. So we continued on during the night, arriving at the apex of the Virgin Mary Hill about midnight. There was fully three feet of snow at that point.

"All the way from Mayer's station to this point Cuddy and the soldiers would pass bottles to each other as they sang ribald ballads, caring nothing for the presence of the only woman aboard, and remonstrating with them had little effect. Cuddy would pass the bottle down to Ned McGowan, each time exclaiming 'and the villain still pursued her!' McGowan was a teetotaler at that time of life, so he would break the partly-filled bottle on the wheel of the coach. A soldier in the stage would pass another bottle to Cuddy, and so it went all during the night. Fortunately, sheer exhaustion overcame Miss McClintock and she slept soundly, thus relieving her from hearing or noting the profanity of the drunken rookies.

"Before commencing the descent of Virgin Mary Hill the driver alighted and made a thorough examination of his brakes and, satisfied of their safety, ascended to his seat, picked up the reins, and cautiously guided the team down the steep grade. It was still snowing so thickly that the lead horse was almost invisible. In a bend of the road about two miles from the summit the driver lost control of the leaders. They shied and, milling on the wheel horses, team, stagecoach and passengers catapulted into a ravine, landing bottom up in a deep snowdrift. The driver, Cuddy, and I were thrown clear of the stage up to our necks in snow. The horses entangled in the traces were floundering around trying to extricate themselves, to the great danger of the passengers in the upturned coach. The driver had the presence of mind to cut the harness, releasing the horses.

"The stagecoach had upset in such a manner that McGowan and Miss McClintock could not be released without serious injury to them, and except for suppressed sobs we were at the moment unable to determine the extent of their injuries. Two of the soldiers were unscathed and they proved to be the only sober ones in the bunch. They say that 'heroes and heroines are born, not made,' and if ever anyone displayed heroics it was Miss Frankie McClintock on this occasion.

"The driver suggested that someone who was able to walk go to Whipple Barracks, notify the commander there, and ask for a rescue party. Cuddy, somewhat sobered by the events, and I started for Whipple, arriving there about four o'clock in the morning. The post was silent as a graveyard when we got there. We were challenged by a sentry and, on stating our mission, were led to the commissary where we wakened the storekeeper, Mr. Oliver. He immediately got in touch with someone in authority, and quickly a detail of soldiers and an ambulance were on the way to the scene of the disaster. Cuddy and I returned with the relief party and assisted in extricating the six partially buried passengers. McGowan was seriously injured, the four soldiers also badly hurt with broken legs and arms, but except for the shock Miss McClintock was uninjured physically. While the relief party was getting the injured passengers out of the upturned coach, Miss McClintock told them, 'Don't mind me; I am all right. Get Judge McGowan and the others out first.' This they had to do, as she was wedged under a seat and McGowan had to be removed before Miss McClintock.

"The injured were taken to the post hospital, and Miss McClintock to Mr. Oliver's residence to recuperate from an attack of nervous prostration. Until the day of her death years later, Frankie McClintock attributed her life to being snugly wrapped up in my 'colchon' and mission blankets. Not only was she kept from freezing to death on the trip, but being wrapped in the bedding it cushioned the jarring of the stage as it struck the bottom of the ravine.

"McGowan never entirely recovered from the injuries he received, but all of us were somewhat compensated by legislative recognition during the session of the 'bloody fighting Thirteenth.' Cuddy was appointed sergeant at arms of the assembly, McGowan a committee clerkship at $6 per diem, and Miss McClintock and I clerkships at six plunks a day. All McGowan ever did for that salary was sign the warrant after adjournment. And so ended one of my most memorable adventures."

Mike Rice mentioned "Virgin Mary Hill", down which the stage trail ran as it approached Prescott from the east, and from which the coach rolled into the ravine. It is the same hill which Barnes mentioned in the previous episode as the six-mile grade the stagecoach climbed as it left Prescott. We still descend it today as we enter Prescott from the east, but instead of the wide, five-lane paved highway we use, it was a narrow, rutted one-lane trail worn into the hillside by repeated travel. It was dusty when it was dry, slippery from mud or ice and snow when it was wet or cold. Obviously, running down it into the town was precarious in good weather but treacherous and dangerous in bad weather.

The name "Virgin Mary Hill" is a reference to one of the first women who lived in Prescott. She was given that venerated nickname because of her many benevolences to the town's early residents. Her real name is said to be Mrs. Cornelius Ramos. The very first building of any kind built in Prescott was a log store and residence, put up at a place called Goose Flat by one Manuel Ysario, a wandering merchant. He arrived with ox teams pulling wagons loaded with goods, and built his store which afterward was known as "Fort Misery." When his stock of goods ran out, Ysario did not replenish it, but moved on, and the cabin was taken over by "Virgin Mary." She ran a boarding house in it for a time, charging her boarders $25 a week in gold in advance. Later, it is said, she owned a ranch on Lynx Creek south of Prescott, where she died and is buried in an unmarked grave.

Rice's reason for referring to the incline as "Virgin Mary Hill" is obscure. The knowledgeable staff of the Sharlot Hall Museum library in Prescott and the courteous forest rangers at the station halfway along the hill state that they have never heard of it in that frame of reference before. So it is most likely that it was because of some incident in Prescott's early history, that time has erased from memory, which caused residents of the town in that era to refer to it by that name.

Travelers along today's Interstate 17 northward from Phoenix can see portions of the old Black Canyon stagecoach trail as they drive. Approaching the community of New River, the old trail can be seen east of the highway coming from Cave Creek and passing the foot of Gavilan (Hawk) Peak. From the New River bridge, the service station said to be built around portions of the old stage station can be seen on the bank of the dry river bed. Some distance on, the freeway crosses the Table Mesa road which ascends into the hills and leads to Tiptop. A little way farther on, Interstate 17 crosses an arroyo which a highway sign says is "Little Squaw Creek." Where this creek joins the Agua Fria River some two or three miles to the west, and on the opposite bank of the Agua Fria, is the location of the old town of Gillett.

Prescott stage station at left end of this picture of Montezuma Street about 1876. (Arizona Historic Photos)

North of Black Canyon City, once called Canon, the highway ascends into the mountains. West of it can be seen portions of the old trail, still in use, on its way to Bumble Bee. From the Sunset Point rest stop at the top of the highway grade, one can see down into the spectacular Agua Fria valley, view the ghost town of Bumble Bee, and see the old Black Canyon stagecoach trail winding into the hills. The road to Prescott leaves the freeway at Cordes Junction, and from Mayer on, the present highway into Prescott follows approximately the route of the old stage road.

The old stagecoach road itself can be traveled most of the way from Phoenix to Prescott. A pick-up truck or four-wheel drive vehicle is almost a necessity. North from Phoenix one begins on the highway to Cave Creek, then takes the old back country desert road from there to New River. From the station there the route follows along to the Table Mesa road, crossing the freeway, and a few miles farther turns into the hills to the north and the ruins of Tiptop strewn along the canyon below the mine. This portion of the road, and that from Tiptop down to the ruins of Gillett on the Agua Fria, has long been abandoned and can only be traveled with great difficulty.

At this point one must cross the Agua Fria to the east side, and by sandy and dusty one-track trails follow along past the Rock Springs store to Black Canyon City. From here the old trail can be followed through the hills to Bumble Bee, and beyond. The precarious ascent is made past the old Cordes ranch to Mayer, and from there follows along the present highway toward Prescott. There is a roadside sign along the highway that says "Old Black Canyon Highway," and points out the old road again. This portion of the stagecoach trail runs south of the highway, through the pines and chaparral for several miles, before rejoining the paved road again a few miles from Prescott.

If you are adventurous and determined enough to ever drive the old Black Canyon stagecoach trail, you will be re-living a memorable era in Arizona. Along those roads the horse teams and mule teams strained and labored, and the stagecoaches creaked and swayed as they rolled. The New River crossing will be dry, but you'll have to ford the Agua Fria which probably won't be. Up the mountainside, you will have to be careful to watch for vehicles going the other way, but you won't hear the strains of the old foghorn to warn you of their approach. The hum of your air conditioner probably would have drowned it out, anyway. But you'll pass the domain of "the prince of station hosts, Joe Mayer," and near the welcome respite of the Bowers Ranch near Dewey. And you won't be alone. The spirits of Captain Gordon and Dave Naegle, of Will Barnes and "Buckey" O'Neill, of Mike Rice and Georgia McClintock, will all be making their memorable journeys with you once again.

Chapter 2

The Bizarre Career of Deputy Marshal Joe Evans

Almost every American knows something of the adventure-filled lives of such Westerners as Buffalo Bill Cody, Bat Masterson, Wyatt Earp, Doc Holliday, and Billy "the Kid" Bonney, all of whom have at least a page in Arizona lore. But for each of the stories of the lives of such famous men, there are many other tales of lives of amazing adventure, experienced by men of the West, of whom few living today have ever heard. One of these is of the dramatic, though short, career of Joe Evans, whose memory time has allowed to slide into an undeserved oblivion. In his day, however, he could be found, if not at the center, then somewhere on the fringe of some of the most sensational events ever to occur in Arizona history.

Joe was born in Cumberland County, North Carolina, on July 4, 1851, the son of Joseph W. and Jane M. Evans. The father died in 1854, when Joe was only three, and by the time he was sixteen years of age young Joe was on his own. No more of his life is known until 1872 when he arrived in Phoenix, in charge of the express business of the Arizona Stage Company in that tiny, sun-baked farming community in the Arizona desert. By 1875 the company had become the California and Arizona Stage Line, operating through Wickenburg and Ehrenberg to San Bernardino, California, and Evans was the agent in charge of the line's Prescott office.

At that time frequent shipments of gold bullion from mines in the Bradshaw Mountains around Prescott were being regularly sent by stage to the San Francisco mint. Consequently the stagecoaches were frequently held up and robbed between

Prescott and Wickenburg, a stretch of the run where the stages going opposite ways passed each other in Peeples Valley. Stage agents and drivers were very conscious of this, and wary. Accounts in the Prescott *Arizona Miner* newspaper on February 19, 1875, and the reminiscences of Arizona pioneer Charles M. Clark record the following event, differing somewhat in detail. The stage, a buckboard, was due to leave Prescott at nine o'clock on the 12th for a night run to Wickenburg with a considerable shipment of gold aboard, and was standing in front of the stage office with the team hitched, the vehicle loaded and ready to go. Agent Joe Evans was waiting alongside for the driver to show up, ready to go with him to the post office and express office to pick up the mail and Wells-Fargo treasure box. Driver Jim Carroll, an experienced man in his early thirties, arrived so drunken that he could scarcely stand up, and when he attempted to climb up to the seat fell over backward to the ground.

According to Clark's version, Evans, seeing the condition Carroll was in, said to him, "You go into my room, and lie down and get sober. I'll take your stock out for you until I meet the stage driver coming this way. Then I will change stock with him and return to Prescott. You can do the same tomorrow night and get your own stock back." Carroll, so besotted that he was stubborn, declared, "No man shall pull a line over my stock." But Evans, who had clashed with Carroll before and there was some ill feeling between them, went back to his room to dress for the road. He came back clad in overcoat, muffler and gloves, and started to climb up into the driver's seat to which Carroll finally had made it.

"If you don't get off," he told Carroll, "I'll put you off." Replied Carroll, "Oh, you'll put me off, even I don't get off?" With that, he jerked out his six-shooter and fired at Evans three times, striking him in the lower left arm (though Clark said "upper right arm"). Evans pulled his own gun and shot Carroll twice through the body. Carroll fell off the seat between the horses, crying, "Let up, Evans, you have got me." He then asked the hostler to get him out from between the horses, and as he did so Evans climbed down. "I'm mighty sorry for this, Jim," he said. "Go to hell," replied Carroll. "I'll get you for this as soon as I can stand up." He raised his gun and fired at Evans again, who shot back, striking Carroll in the head.

Evans, badly wounded himself, stumbled back through the stage office to his room behind it and collapsed unconscious on the floor. A growing crowd attracted to the scene by the shooting picked up Carroll and carried him into the building, where they laid him on the floor of the hall just outside Evans' door. Evans said later that when he recovered consciousness on the floor of his room, unable to get to his bed, he knew that he had been hit a number of times and believed that he was dying. But, as he heard Carroll gasping for breath on the floor of the hall just outside his room, he determined that he would not give up until Carroll had quit breathing. "I was never so satisfied in my life," he said later, "as when Carroll choked, gurgled, and I knew he had breathed his last breath."

In the meantime, a doctor had been summoned from Fort Whipple. He helped Evans remove his clothing and get into bed. It was found that Carroll's shots had hit Evans several times in the left arm. The doctor could hear what was going on outside, where a number of Carroll's friends had the crowd clamoring for a rope to lynch Evans. Having stopped Evans' bleeding from his wounds, the doctor stepped outside into the hall. "Please be quiet, men," he said. "Mr. Evans is about to die. I am sure you do not wish to lynch a dying man." At this, having found that Carroll had quit breathing, and upon further assurances from the doctor that Evans could not live through the night, the crowd dispersed.

As soon as the last of them had gone, the doctor, assisted by one of the hostlers, carried Evans out to his military ambulance and took him to the hospital at Fort Whipple. Coroner Henry Bigelow held an inquest, and the coroner's jury returned the verdict in Carroll's demise of "Death from a pistol shot fired by the hand of J. W. Evans." Asked by the coroner to express their opinion as to whether the killing was justifiable or not, the jury declined to do so, and was discharged. According to the *Weekly Miner* of March 5, 1875, Evans' life was saved from an infection that threatened it, but his left arm had to be amputated at the shoulder.

There seems to be no record of any other official hearing or action taken in this gun duel. Evans eventually completely recovered—other than the loss of his left arm at the age of twenty-four—and went back to work. The Arizona Miner in its August 21, 1877, issue mentioned him as the principal witness in the trial of stage robbers Vance and Berry. Evans was a passenger on a stagecoach on the Tonto Springs road in the spring of that year, when it was held up by two men. After the robbers had left, Evans obtained a horse, returned quickly to Prescott and notified Town Marshal Standefer. Together they started out on the road, where they surprised the robbers casually riding into town. Arrested and found with some of the stage passengers' personal property in their possession, Vance and Berry had come up with the lame excuse that a man on horseback had overtaken them and just gave them the money and property. Though Evans was in San Francisco for some reason, the trial went on, doubtless with disastrous results for the robbers, caught red-handed.

San Francisco was the western headquarters for the renowned Wells-Fargo Express Company, and it was in that year, 1877, that Evans left the C&A Stage Line to become a special agent for Wells-Fargo. He was also about this same time appointed a United States Deputy Marshal, and held down both positions at the same time. As a matter of history, the Arizona territorial capital, which had been at Tucson from 1866 until 1876, was moved back to Prescott in 1876. Apparently United States Marshal Crawley P. Dake remained in Tucson, but needed a deputy at the state capital, and Joe Evans, with a solid reputation in Prescott as fearless and capable, would be a natural as an appointee and assistant there to the U. S. Marshal himself.

In his capacity as a Wells-Fargo special agent, Evans was involved in a remarkable incident in mid-1878. It was re-told in the reminiscences of Arizona pioneer Charles M. Clark. "In Tucson, George Fields, who had previously owned one of the largest wagon freighting outfits on the road between Yuma and Tucson, was operating a livery and feed corral in 1876," wrote Clark (though the date was actually 1878). "Working for Fields at this time as boss of the hay teams was a man by the name of James Brazelton, a long, lanky, loose-jointed, big-boned Missourian, good-natured, a good mixer, and a generally all-around good fellow.

"Brazelton bore an excellent reputation, and was well liked, and when he rounded up his crew of Papagos with their grub hoes, and started out to load his wagons with 'galleta' or 'sacaton,' (types of wild grasses), there was a cheery 'Good luck, Jim' extended by every one who he met. Fields was paying Brazelton sixty dollars per month and board. On his salary, with the prevalent attractions of Tucson, and many excuses for keeping legal tender in circulation, Brazelton could not lay by much money. The road to independence, with an outfit of his own, seemed interminably long. He wanted very much to make one trip back to his home town, and be able to 'show them a good time' when he got there. But on sixty and beans, this was impossible.

"Telling Fields that he was going back to Missouri, he resigned his job as hay boss and disappeared. Within a day or two thereafter, the stage coming from Florence to Tucson was held up at Point of Mountain, a few miles north of Tucson. The following night the stage was held up at the same place. In each case the Wells-Fargo box was taken, and the passengers lined up alongside the road and compelled to deposit their valuables in the roadway at their feet.

"Joe W. Evans, formerly stage agent at Prescott where he lost his right arm in a gun fight, had established his reputation as a cool and fearless fighter, and had been appointed as chief messenger for the Territory of Arizona by the Wells-Fargo Express Company. When the second holdup had occurred at Point of Mountain, Evans was ordered to the scene of the robbery to 'ride the stage' and get the robber. Before Evans could get to Florence to take the stage for Tucson, the stage was again held up at the same place. In each instance, the drivers reported that the man who held them up was armed with a fifty caliber Sharp's carbine, with a .45 Colt strapped to each side of the carbine, that he was a very large man, and very cool about his work.

"Reaching Florence, Evans boarded the stage for Tucson, leaving in the evening for the all-night ride to Tucson. As the Concord stage clicked its way along the road, Evans interrogated the driver as to the circumstances and 'modus operandi' of the various holdups. Along about four o'clock in the morning,

Evans asked the driver where it was that he was held up, and the driver replied, 'Right down the road here a little ways.' Shortly afterward, he turned to Evans who was riding on the seat beside him, and, pointing to a big boulder alongside the road, said, 'Night before last, he was right behind that rock.'

"At this the robber stepped into the road saying, 'Yep, and I am here again. Drop that box, and line up, everybody.' His Sharp's carbine-two .45 arsenal pointed directly at Evans who, with the two inside passengers, descended into the road. Evans was requested to drop his gun to the ground at his feet. Evans had a fine gold watch which had been presented to him by the Wells-Fargo company, properly inscribed, as a reward for bravery, and he did not like the idea of losing it. Remonstrating with the robber but to no avail, his gun, watch, and money were added to those of the two passengers. Then the driver was ordered to 'drive on,' leaving the Wells-Fargo treasure box where he had dropped it at the first command of the robber.

"Reaching Tucson about seven o'clock in the morning, Evans secured breakfast, and at once organized a posse, including two Papago Indian trailers, and returned to the scene of the robbery. Taking up the trail of the robber's horse, it was followed around the west side of Tucson and finally lost in the big forest of mesquite trees which then existed between Tucson and the Mission San Xavier. After spending the day in futile efforts to pick up the trial, Evans and his posse returned to Tucson, intending to return the following day to again search for the trail.

"The following morning, when the stage from Florence arrived at Tucson, the driver reported being held up again at the same place, and by the same man with his Sharp's carbine and two six-guns. Immediately after the arrival of the stage, Evans and posse, with the two trailers, went to the scene of the robbery, where they again took the trail. Following it to the mesquite forest, it was again lost as on the preceding day.

"Charlie Shibbell was the sheriff of Pima County at that time and, acting upon information given him by Evans the previous day, set his local organization at work. He found that every afternoon about three o'clock a certain Mexican of questionable reputation left Tucson, returning after dark. Putting a Papago Indian trailer upon the Mexican's trail, Shibbell, with a small but determined posse, followed the Indian at a distance. Reaching the edge of the mesquite forest on the east, opposite to the point where Evans and the posse entered it, the Indian was waiting for Shibbell and said, 'Him puttem grub on a log.'

"Shibbell and two of his men crept into the grove behind the Indian a short distance, to where the Indian pointed to a big fallen mesquite log, upon which were several bundles wrapped in grain sacks. Lying quiet, screened by the underbrush, Shibbell and his men waited about an hour, when Jim Brazelton appeared cautiously approaching the log. When he reached it, he unwrapped one of the bundles and began eating. Shibbell then shouted, 'Stick 'em up, Jim!' But when Brazelton's hands came up, they carried the well-described Sharp's carbine, with a .45 strapped to each side of it.

"At this movement on the part of Brazelton, one of the deputies let go with both barrels of a sawed-off shotgun loaded with buckshot. And Jim Brazelton resigned all hope of a trip back home in Missouri and a good time with the old bunch. He died where he fell. When the posse finally found his hangout, they found several hundred dollars in money, a number of rings and watches, and a brand new saddle which the Mexican who had furnished Brazelton with food, said he had purchased at Brazelton's request. Jim had made his last holdup, and intended starting the following day for Paso del Norte (El Paso), en route to Missouri, and a good time with the old bunch."

For some months prior to, and for a period immediately after the preceding incident, Evans was deeply involved as part of his duties as a U. S. Deputy Marshal in the bewildering events leading to the death of Jack Swilling, an Arizona pioneer known to almost everyone in the territory, in a Yuma prison. Swilling, one of the founders of Phoenix in 1870, was by 1878 living in the Black Canyon country north of that town. The owners of the Tiptop Mine chose a site on the Agua Fria River in the Black Canyon, eight miles below the mine, on which to build an ore mill and town. Swilling moved his headquarters to the new town, named Gillett. In April, 1878, at the suggestion of his wife, Swilling with two friends, Andrew Kirby and George Munroe, traveled to White Picacho southeast of Wickenburg, to unearth the remains of a friend who had been killed there by Indians, and bring the body back to Gillett for a Christian burial.

While they were on this mission, a stagecoach was robbed near Wickenburg, and the mail sacks, the Wells-Fargo box containing gold and silver bullion, and gold coins obtained from the passengers were taken. Having returned from his journey, bringing back the remains of his friend, Swilling was drinking in a Gillett saloon when he jokingly boasted that it was he,

Arizona Pioneer Jack Swilling, arrested by Evans and sent to a Yuma jail where he died. Note gun in hand resting on shoulder. (Arizona Historical Society)

Kirby and Munroe who had robbed the stagecoach. Some enemies of Swilling overhead this, and had Swilling and Kirby arrested. The arresting officer was Joe Evans. The two men and Munroe were taken to Prescott, where they were indicted for the crime by a grand jury. Munroe made bond and was released, but Swilling and Kirby failed to make bond and were held in jail. Then it was found that the robbery had taken place in Maricopa County, in the Third Judicial District, not in Yavapai County in the First Judicial District which included Prescott.

Proceedings against the accused men had to be re-instituted in either Phoenix or Yuma, both in the Third District. On June 16, 1878, for some reason Evans secretly had Swilling and Kirby transferred by stagecoach to Yuma, where another hearing was held. Still Swilling and Kirby were held in prison, neither able to make the bond set at $3,000. Under this stress and already in poor health, Swilling died in Yuma prison on August 12th.

Then, on September 2nd, another robbery occurred in which the mail and Wells-Fargo box were taken along with the passengers' valuables. There were some suspects in this holdup, named Rhodes, Rondepaugh (or Rodenpaugh) and Mullen, and having received a tip on Rhodes' whereabouts, Evans set out on his trail. Nothing was heard from him for a time, but on September 21, 1878, an article appeared in the *Arizona Sentinel,* a Yuma newspaper: "Andrew Kirby, who lies in Yuma jail on a charge of stage robbery, on Thursday received a telegram from George Munroe who is under bonds on the same charge, stating that Deputy Marshal Evans had that morning left Tucson for Yuma with Rhodes, whom he had in custody. Kirby, Swilling and Munroe have always claimed that Rhodes and two others were the parties who really committed the crime for which they were arrested. The capture of Rhodes may lead to establishing the innocence of Kirby and Munroe. It is believed that Rhodes' partners have also been captured."

A week later, on September 28, the *Sentinel* carried the story of how "Rhodes," an alias for a man named Stout, had been captured by Evans. "John S. Stout, alias Rhodes and other names, was lodged in Yuma jail last Saturday by Deputy

Marshal Evans and Special Mail Agent Mahoney. . . The above named officers first heard of his having been at Rio Mimbres, New Mexico, after committing the (September 2nd) robbery and of his probably having left there for Arizona. Evans went over there, while Mahoney remained in Arizona to follow any clues telegraphed by Evans. The latter followed traces of Stout over to Silver City, to Fort Cummings and back, toward Clifton and back, toward Pueblo Viejo (Solomonville) and finally to a point about fifteen miles above Camp Thomas (later Fort Thomas) on the Gila River. . .

"Stout had broken up his share of the stolen silver bullion and had sold the pieces at various points, thus scattering sure traces of his course. When captured he was driving a herd of cattle for Van Smith. Evans rode up to the herd, and asked for Stout, who was pointed out to him. He then rode up to him and said, 'Good morning.' Then quickly covering him, he made him alight, threw him a pair of handcuffs, made him put them on, mount his horse again, and trot down the road toward Camp Thomas before any of the other herders had an opportunity to know what was going on. That morning Stout's back had hurt him, and he had taken off his pistols and left them in the mess wagon. . ."

Evans obtained a confession from Stout, alias Rhodes, that he and his two companions had committed both the September 2nd robbery and that for which Swilling and his friends had been charged. He notified the authorities in Yuma that Kirby's innocence had been established, and Kirby was released from custody. Understandably incensed over his long incarceration on what proved to be a false charge, Kirby remained in Yuma, drinking and issuing threats against all law officers, especially Joe Evans. When he arrived in Yuma with Rhodes in tow, Evans was warned that Kirby was still in town, and had threatened to kill him.

Learning in which saloon Kirby was drinking, Evans hunted him up. Kirby was at the bar when Evans entered. "I hear you're going to kill me," said Evans. "Yes," replied Kirby. "Well, get ready," Evans told him, covering him with his six-gun. "Don't shoot," cried out Kirby. "I've got no gun. Don't kill an unarmed man." Evans laid his revolver on a table. "Kirby," he said, "we must have this thing out. There's my gun. I'll be back in a few minutes and will begin shooting as soon as I see you." And Evans walked out.

When he returned in a few minutes with another gun, Kirby was gone. Evans left word for him that he would be shot on sight, and Kirby left town at once. Several years later the two men met again in a store at Arivaca. On this occasion Kirby tried to stab Evans, but was held off at the point of a gun.

At the trial of Stout, or Rhodes, Evans recommended leniency, probably because of his confession and co-operation with the authorities in waiving extradition, and he was sentenced to nine years in prison. After serving six years, Stout was pardoned at the intercession again of Joe Evans. He promised to stay away from Arizona, but came back later on and was arrested for drunkenness in Tucson. Again at Evans' intercession, he was released on condition that he leave the Territory. Neither of his accomplices in the robberies was ever apprehended, though on two occasions Evans made trips to other states where authorities believed they had one of the men in custody.

One of the most sensational incidents in the history of Arizona Territory occurred in August, 1883, and again Joe Evans as a U. S. Deputy Marshal was at the center of it. The incident was the lynching of Len Redfield and Joe Tuttle, suspected of complicity in a stage robbery, in the town of Florence. The robbery itself was pulled off just east of Riverside Station on the road from Florence to Globe, in which shotgun guard Johnnie Collins was killed and the Wells-Fargo treasure box looted. The robbers fled along the Gila River until they reached its tributary, the San Pedro River, and continued down the San Pedro closely followed by a posse under Pinal County Sheriff Jim Doran.

At Redfield's Ranch on the San Pedro, the posse uncovered evidence that the ranch was the hideout for a gang of highwaymen, and that Len Redfield was one of the gang's masterminds. Len Redfield and a man named Joe Tuttle, suspected of being one of the actual robbers of the stage, were arrested and brought back to Florence where they were lodged in a jail cell in the old

Pinal County courthouse. The arrest of Len Redfield caused a sensation in the entire territory, as he was a respected rancher running hundreds of cattle over a large range. Few of the more prominent people believed that Redfield was guilty, or involved in stagecoach robberies in any way.

The citizens of the town of Florence, however, were deeply incensed over the crime, especially the murder of Johnnie Collins. There was open talk in the streets of vigilante action. Of the several accounts of the robbery and its aftermath, perhaps the most reliable is that by Mike M. Rice, pioneer Arizona newspaperman and sometimes law officer, who was a deputy sheriff in Florence at the time and an eyewitness to the events in Florence. "There was at the time, and for several years afterward, a well-organized Vigilance Committee in Florence," goes Mike's account, "but up to this time their main function was the notifying of undesirables to quit the town.

"Redfield had a brother in Benson, a prominent business-man and much respected citizen. When he learned of his brother's arrest and that his life was threatened by the vigilantes, he immediately came to Phoenix, went before Judge W. Wood Porter, and secured a writ of habeas corpus to produce the prisoners in Phoenix. The writ was handed to U. S. Deputy Marshal Evans for service on the sheriff of Pinal County. While Evans was a fearless man and a good officer, he lacked judgment and diplomacy." It should be noted that the preceding assessment of Evans' competency is a direct quote from Mike Rice, whose close contact with the situation may have colored his thinking, and whose opinion may not have been held by everyone else.

"Evans took the train to Casa Grande," continues Mike's account, "and here heard that the people of Florence objected to the removal of Redfield and Tuttle from the jurisdiction of Pinal County. Evans boasted of his authority as a United States official, and that he intended taking the prisoners at any cost, so he unwisely swore in a posse of saloon loafers in Casa Grande to assist him in serving the writ and securing the prisoners." Other accounts differ with Rice's description of Evans' posse. Sheriff Jim Doran called them "nine noted gunmen," and historian James Barney actually named the men as Paddy

Burke, Louis LePage, Ballock, Johnson, and Redfield's brother, sent with Evans under order of the court to act as guards while Len Redfield and Tuttle were being transferred to Phoenix.

The fact that Evans was en route to Florence with a posse backing him, went on Mike Rice's account, "was wired to the leader of the vigilantes, and they prepared to give Mr. Evans and his posse a reception. When Evans reached Florence, he went with his squad to the courthouse and there served the writ on Undersheriff Scanlan (Sheriff Doran being out of town at the time), who sought the advice of District Attorney Jesse Hardesty, as the crime was not committed on a United States, military, or Indian reservation. Mr. Hardesty advised against honoring the writ, as the case legally belonged to the territory and county. At this point Evans got on his high horse and gave Scanlan just ten

Pinal County Courthouse in Florence as it originally appeared. Sheriff's office was on ground floor at the extreme left. (Courtesy Pinal County Historical Society)

minutes to produce the prisoners, otherwise he would break down the doors and take them by force.

"While this short parley was going on, the Vigilance Committee were also busy. They entered the jail yard by a rear gate, reached the cell block, dragged Redfield and Tuttle from their cells, and hanged them from the rafters in the jail corridor. This was done so quietly that Evans and his crowd in the sheriff's office did not hear what was happening in the jail, so they proceeded to break the door leading from the sheriff's office to the jail corridor. 'Hold on, Evans!' said the undersheriff. 'Don't destroy county property. I will open the doors,' and he did so, saying, 'Here's your prisoners.' And there they were, the first and only unlawful execution ever pulled off in Pinal County." Mike Rice was wrong about that. Florence, maybe, but not all of Pinal County.

"Some people," wrote Mike Rice in conclusion, "said that Undersheriff Scanlan was cognizant beforehand that a lynching was to be pulled off, and that he made no effort to protect his charges. He was accused by the cowboy element of being an accessory before the fact, and it worked great injury to one of the most efficient peace officers of Arizona. Sheriff Jim Doran came up for re-election and was defeated by the cattlemen's vote because he retained Scanlan in office after the lynching. . ."

Evans also made a "walk-on appearance" in the Tombstone drama of Wyatt Earp and his brothers. The "gunfight at the O. K. Corral" occurred on October 26, 1881, in Tombstone. In it Billy Clanton and Tom and Frank McLowery were shot dead by Town Marshal Virgil Earp and by Wyatt Earp, Morgan Earp and Doc Holliday acting as deputies to Virgil. In retaliation, the outlaw element, of which the slain men had been prominent members, let it be known that it had a "hit list." On it, marked for assassination, were the Earps and Holliday, Mayor John Clum, Attorney Tom Fitch who had defended Wyatt at his hearing, and Justice of the Peace Wells Spicer who had dismissed the charges against the Earps and Holliday, and others.

In December, an attempt was made to assassinate Mayor Clum, but he escaped. On the night of December 28th, five men firing from ambush with shotguns tried to kill Virgil Earp on the street between the Oriental Saloon and the Crystal Palace. Virgil escaped death, but his left arm was maimed by shotgun pellets. Then on the night of March 17, 1882, Morgan Earp was shot in the back through the glass panes of a rear door as he was playing a game in Hatch's pool parlor. He died a few hours later, and Wyatt Earp received a tip that the assassin was Frank Stilwell.

Morgan's body was sent to Colton, California, where the Earp brothers' parents were living, for burial. The maimed

Virgil, not yet fully recovered from his wounds, started by rail for Colton escorted by Wyatt and Doc Holliday, who wanted to accompany him as far as Tucson to discourage further attempts on his life by the outlaws. Beyond Tucson, they felt he would be safe. As the train rolled westward from Benson, a little distance before arriving at Tucson the train paused and a U. S. Deputy Marshal got on with a warning. Frank Stilwell and other outlaws were in Tucson, they had received telegrams that the Earps and Holliday were on the train, and Sheriff Bob Paul was out of town. The Earps and Doc Holliday would have to be vigilant and take care of themselves. The U. S. Deputy, who had only one arm, was Joe Evans.

Thus warned, Wyatt Earp and Doc Holliday patrolled the station platform in Tucson while Virgil remained on the train. In doing so, they spotted a man lurking in the railroad yard, watching for the train to pull out. Earp and Holliday ran down the side of a string of boxcars opposite the man, and at its end confronted him. The next morning he was found dead, face down in the yard, his body riddled by four six-gun bullets and two shotgun blasts. It was Frank Stilwell.

Sometime in his career Evans acquired the title of "Major." Just how or when is obscure, as he never served in the military. Perhaps his friends dubbed him that, or he may have arrogated it to himself, as was common on the frontier. Men who had no right to use some title took it anyway, to add to their prestige. This was especially true of the title "judge," often appropriated by men who had never seen a law book. So maybe Joe felt his name needed a little more weight and picked out a title he liked.

In 1885, at the age of thirty-four, Evans retired as a U. S. Deputy Marshal and embarked in the real estate and loan business in Phoenix. He was very successful and became a prominent businessman, the second president of the Phoenix Chamber of Commerce. A biographical history of prominent men in the territory in 1896 said, "His office, 20 x 70 feet, occupies one of the most conspicuous corners in the city," which was the southwest corner of Central and Washington. "He owns fruit, alfalfa, and grain ranches in the east, north, and north-west parts of the valley," it stated, and listed him as president of five canal and farm companies and a director of two others.

And, "he was married June 30, 1896, to Mrs. Sarah Gertrude Lee in Detroit, Michigan."

So the fiery warrior retired from the deputy marshal's life of privation and danger to that of the wealthy and respected businessman, a familiar figure along the valley roads behind a team of spirited horses. He died in Phoenix on May 28, 1902. Some men reading about his exciting life now, after a hundred years, may experience a disturbing emotion. It's known as "envy."

Chapter 3

The Saga of Inez & Josefa

In September, 1849, a group of pilgrims left their homes in the town of Santa Cruz in northern Mexico to attend the feast of Our Lady of Magdalena and to visit the grave of Father Kino in Magdalena, a town about fifteen miles distant and a two-day journey. Kino was once a Catholic priest sainted by the church for his missionary work among the Mexican peasants. In the party of pilgrims were a beautiful fifteen-year-old girl, Inez Gonzales, her aunt, uncle, cousin, and a girlfriend, Josefa Salvador. They were accompanied by an escort of ten soldiers, since the road led through the deep, rugged Cocospero Canyon where there were springs that were also used by the fierce Apache Indians.

In the canyon the pilgrims were attacked by Pinal Apaches. All the pilgrims and the escort of soldiers were murdered except for Inez and Josefa who were carried away to become Apache slaves. Josefa was claimed by an Apache warrior, Maht-la, as his wife, of which much more is to be recounted later in this tale. Inez, however, was held in Apache captivity, somewhat protected by an old squaw who for some reason had befriended her. Inez still was forced to do menial chores around the camps and help gather roots and seeds for food.

In June of the following year, 1850, U.S. Capt. John Cremony was attached to the joint U.S.-Mexican boundary commission, at its headquarters at the Santa Rita copper mines near today's Silver City, New Mexico. He noticed one evening that a campfire was burning a short distance away in an area where camps were forbidden. He and a companion walked up to the fire unnoticed and found there a beautiful Mexican girl cooking food. They tried to talk to her, but she hurried away evidently in great fear. When she returned, they persuaded her to talk, and found that she had been captured by the Apaches and sold to slave traders.

The slave traders were Mexicans who roamed northern Mexico capturing, or purchasing from the Apaches, attractive young girls whom they took to a slave market in Santa Fe, New Mexico, and sold them to unscrupulous buyers for whatever purposes they had in mind. Cremony and his companion hurried to lay the matter before the American chief of the boundary commission, John Bartlett, who ordered soldiers to be sent immediately to rescue her. She was brought before Bartlett who, after hearing her story, gave her sanctuary and the best of care.

The slave traders were given a hearing, but as Bartlett had no power to hold them he had to release them. The rest of the commission, however, outraged, told them to get lost, and quickly, or face the punishment they deserved. They hurriedly decamped and were gone in twenty minutes.

The rescued girl was, of course, Inez Gonzales. There are differing reports of the next episode in her life. One is that she was restored to her family in Santa Cruz; another is that she was taken to the Mexican governmental headquarters at Tubac, then part of Sonora, and turned over to the governor there, Capt. Gomez, to be returned to her family. Whichever is the case, Inez attracted the attention of Capt. Gomez who fell in

Tubac, 1864, from a sketch by J. Ross Browne in his book "Adventures in the Apache Country." (Arizona Historical Society.)

love with her. She remained at his home for some years and bore him two sons, though Gomez had a wife in Mexico City. Eventually Gomez' wife divorced him, and Inez and Gomez were married.

In time, Gomez died and Inez returned to Santa Cruz. There she met and married the alcalde, or mayor, of the town and Inez had another son and daughter. In 1862 Capt. Cremony, who had rescued her from the slave traders and in whose reminiscences most of this account is found, was a soldier in the Union's California Column. It was sent from California across Arizona toward New Mexico to drive out the Confederates as the Civil War was then being fought. Hearing that Cremony was in Tucson, Inez wrote to him, saying that she was not well, and begging him to send an army physician to attend and prescribe for her. Unable to do so, Cremony put it out of his mind.

In 1864 Cremony was in command of troops who pursued some Mexican soldiers into Mexico after they had made an incursion into U.S. territory and fired on American citizens at San Gabriel (now known as Lochiel). They chased them all the way back to Magdalena. Coming back, Cremony visited Inez in Santa Cruz, where he found her in good health again, surrounded by a loving family and with a well-to-do husband.

Meanwhile, what of Josefa Salvador who had been captured by the Apaches at the same time as Inez? It was some months before Cremony's soldiers, begged by the citizens of Santa Cruz to rescue her, were able to locate her in Chief Paramuca's band ranging in the Sonoita-Patagonia mountains. Forced into marriage with Maht-la she was now heavy with child. Cremony was able to effect her release, however, and she remained with the boundary commission as she was an orphan and unwilling to return to Santa Cruz in her condition. Bartlett allowed her to stay and assigned the commission's doctor, Dr. T. H. Webb, to care for her.

In October, 1851, shortly before she was to give birth, Josefa disappeared. A month later she re-appeared with her baby, a son, in an Apache cradleboard. He had been born on the dirt floor of a wickiup in the hills along the border. The baby's left eye was swollen and partially covered with a mucous-like growth. Dr. Webb concluded that something, possibly a grain of sand, had lodged between the eye and eyelid at birth. He did what he could, but did not attempt to remove the growth.

As suddenly as she had disappeared in October from the commission's camp, Josefa disappeared again in January, 1852, this time to go to Tucson looking for a doctor for her baby's eye. Unable to find help for him, she somehow made a living for a year when she found work as a Spanish-American interpreter for the boundary commission. During this period there had been a change, however; the commission was now commanded by Major William H. Emory who would finish its work. Josefa transferred to the U.S. Indian Bureau's office in Tucson, but when the Bureau wanted to send her to Yuma that was too much for her. South of Tucson the former seat of Mexican government at Tubac was now an American possession, and was the headquarters of a mining operation headed by the celebrated "Father of Arizona," Charles D. Poston. Josefa wound up working for Poston.

Poston also ran the sutler's store at Fort Buchanan, eastward from Tubac over the Santa Rita Mountains and not far from where Josefa had been held an Apache captive and where her son had been born. In 1859 Josefa was clerking in Poston's sutler's store at Fort Buchanan, where she met a rancher named John Ward. He had originally been a member of Poston's mining company, but had now gone to ranching, and

Mickey Free, U. S. Army scout and interpreter during the Apache campaigns. (Bureau of American Ethnology)

had built up a successful operation. Josefa agreed to move into his ranch house on Sonoita Creek with him, their arrangement at last providing her and her son a measure of security.

Josefa's boy, now eight years old, had an Apache name, Migga-n'a-la-iae, but it was too much for Ward who called him Mickey. The couple got along well together for about a year when Ward came back from a trip to Tubac in December, 1860, and found that in his absence Apaches had raided the ranch and run off most of his stock, cattle and horses. And they had kidnapped his stepson, Josefa's cock-eyed boy, Mickey. Josie was devastated, but she had recognized the raiders as Pinal Apaches, of the same clan in which she had been held captive.

Though the Pinal Apaches regularly raided this area along the border, killing, looting and plundering as was the Apaches' inbred way of life, their homeland was in the Pinal Mountains of central Arizona which now overlook the towns of Globe and Miami. Driving Ward's stock, they fled toward their homeland. Ward, following, decided that Josefa had been mistaken and that the raiders were Chiricahua Apaches whose chief was the

Ruins of historic Butterfield stage station in Apache Pass where Lt. George Bascom and the Apache Chief Cochise had their confrontation in 1861.

great Cochise. The trail led in the direction of the Chiricahua Mountains. Finding it too dangerous to follow the trail any farther alone, Ward returned to Fort Buchanan to seek help from the military.

Ward kept after the post commander until finally he sent a detail of soldiers to try to find the boy. It was commanded by a young lieutenant, George Bascom, not long out of West Point and unfamiliar with Apache ways. Bascom set out with his sixteen men, and Ward as the trail guide, on January 28, 1861. They proceeded to Apache Pass in the Chiricahua Mountains, passed the Butterfield Overland Stage station, and camped in Siphon Draw about a mile from the famed Apache Spring in the pass. A squaw at the station took the news to Chief Cochise, camped in the hills above the pass, and Cochise, unaware of Bascom's mission, decided to visit him.

Cochise was then at peace with the Americans, having made an agreement with the Butterfield officials who furnished him with trade goods and paid his people for furnishing firewood to the stage station. With two nephews, a brother, wife and a child, he paid Bascom a social call. Unknown to Cochise, when they entered Bascom's tent, it was immediately surrounded by soldiers. Bascom stated his mission, and Cochise replied that he knew nothing of the stolen stock or the boy, said that the raid might have been the work of Pinal or Coyotero Apaches, and offered to find out and try to have the captive returned.

Bascom then made the first of a series of terrible mistakes. He accused Cochise of lying and said he and his relatives would be held hostage until the boy was returned. Cochise suddenly slashed through the tent with a knife hidden in his breech clout, escaped untouched by the hail of bullets, and by signal fires called in his warriors. Bascom moved his camp to the stage station. Cochise managed to capture three of the station employees and offered to exchange them for his relatives held by the soldiers. Bascom replied there would be no exchange that did not include the boy, whereupon Cochise had his hostages killed. The Apaches also attacked a wagon train in the pass, looted it, and tortured and burned everyone to death.

Bascom sent for reinforcements, which arrived and aided in

Remains of King Woolsey's ranchhouse in 2000, on the Agua Fria River near Dewey. From here began the expedition against the Apaches that ended at the Battle of Bloody Tanks.

a search for Cochise, which, of course, was futile. As they withdrew to return to their post, the soldiers in retaliation for the captives killed by Cochise, hanged his male relatives, sparing only the woman and her child. Cochise bitterly declared war on all Americans, a war that lasted twelve years. In that time no stagecoach or wagon train ever moved through Apache pass without an armed escort. All of this was caused by one nine-year-old, half-Mexican and half-Apache boy.

Later in the year 1861 the Civil War began, and the soldiers at frontier outposts were called east to fight in that great war. Fort Buchanan, and nearly all other Arizona military forts, was burned to the ground with all its supplies as the soldiers withdrew. The Apaches, watching this, thought they had won their battle to drive out the hated white men, and stepped up their raids on the remaining ranches and settlements. Everyone had to flee to some protection from the rampaging warriors. John Ward and Josefa were among them, probably going to Tucson. Josefa never again saw her son, held in Chief Paramuca's band of the Pinal Apaches.

Because of the Civil War, the Butterfield Overland company went out of business. Some of its stations were taken over and put back in service for other stage lines. One of them was Stanwick's Station, on the Gila River west of today's Gila Bend. The new owner was a famous Arizonan, King Woolsey, who built a ranch at Agua Caliente across the river from Stanwick's. Woolsey started up another ranch on the Agua Fria River, far to the north near today's town of Dewey, south of the city of Prescott. In January, 1864, Pinal Apaches raided the ranches in that area, driving off stock, some of which belonged to Woolsey. He immediately volunteered to lead a party of ranchers to pursue the raiders, recover the stock if possible, and punish the Indians.

Woolsey led his party of twenty-eight men down the Black Canyon where today's highway runs, then across the desert eastward, north of where the city of Phoenix would arise. Supplies began to run low, so some of the men went to the stage station at Maricopa Wells on the old Butterfield Stage route for replenishment. They returned with supplies, and with fourteen Maricopa Indian warriors, hereditary enemies of the Apaches. The party regrouped at the junction of the Salt and Verde Rivers. A few days later the pursuers found themselves in mountainous country at the edge of some rock "tanks," and stopped to cook breakfast.

No sooner had they started fires when the hills around began to blaze with answering fires. Woolsey's men had found the Apaches, more than they had expected. Confident of victory in the battle to come, the Pinal Apaches under Chief Paramuca taunted the white men. "We are your enemies!" they shouted. "We have stolen your horses and cattle, we have killed you whenever we could, and will continue to kill you whenever we meet you. If you are not squaws, come on and fight us!"

The Apaches agreed to a parley, but before going to the talk Woolsey instructed his men that if a fight became inevitable he would touch the brim of his hat, a signal to begin shooting immediately. Chief Paramuca came into camp, haughtily demanding that a place be smoothed in the sand for him to sit. Woolsey instead handed him a blanket, which Paramuca reluctantly laid on the ground and sat down.

The parley went badly; Paramuca made demands impossible to fulfill. Woolsey touched his hat, at the same time drawing his pistol and killing Paramuca on the spot. Others of the party immediately began firing at the completely surprised Apaches. They fled the parley completely disorganized, and most of them were killed in the battle that lasted only seven or eight minutes. This is known as the "Battle of Bloody Tanks," because the water running through the rock "tanks" was said to have been red with blood. The location of this fight is somewhere near today's town of Miami.

We have not departed from our story of Josefa's boy, Mickey, however. He was at the "Battle of Bloody Tanks," left with some squaws to hold the horses while the Apaches fought. After the battle Mickey escaped and eventually made his way back to the south, now completely on his own, though he was only thirteen years old. He came again to the old Butterfield Overland Stage road. A freight outfit was traveling on it, somehow surviving despite the Apache rampage, operating between El Paso and Yuma by way of Tucson. A part-owner, Willy Freeman, was in charge.

Mickey stayed on with the freight outfit, as help was hard to come by, and he quickly demonstrated that he could handle teams of horses and mules. Moreover, he was bright, agreeable, and willing to work. He caught on with Willy Freeman and stayed two years, working for food, clothing and shelter—and gained something of much more value. Freeman taught him English, thus making him one of the few people on the frontier conversant in three languages, English, Mexican and Apache. He also gave Mickey a knife that was primarily a dagger, and he soon learned its deadly uses.

U. S. Army officer with line of Apaches recruited to be Army scouts. (Bureau of American Ethnology)

Freeman's outfit had to fight off occasional Apache attacks, but there was another danger on the road. Bands of Mexican banditos were a constant threat, who did their dirty work and usually it was blamed on the Indians. They attacked Freeman's train on the Tubac-Tucson road, Willy was killed, Mickey was wounded but managed to escape with his life. Feeling his loss of a friend, Mickey took Willy's name and became Mickey

Mickey Free, U. S. Army scout and interpreter, posed for this picture during an official visit to Washington, D.C. (Bureau of American Ethnology)

Freeman, which over time shortened to just Mickey Free. Somewhere he found shelter while he recuperated, on his own again at seventeen.

For the next couple of years, Mickey worked for an American in Sonora, Mexico, who employed a force of mixed nationalities in an excavation project, and needed a man who spoke the languages and could help handle the volatile workers. He learned to use his knife with deadly precision, finding the results just as useful as when he employed a gun, but without the sounds that accompanied shots. When some of the workers tried to take over the payroll, Mickey sided with his employer in the shootout but the man was killed. Then the workers came after him but Mickey, in Apache fashion, simply faded away, and in time returned to the United States.

Someone suggested to Mickey that he would fit in well with the Apache scouts being recruited for service in the U.S. army during the Apache wars. He traveled to Fort Whipple near Prescott to consult a man he trusted, to inquire about his mother, and to find whether his nationality was Apache, Mexican or American. He was informed that he would be considered an American, and sadly told that his mother had died about a year ago and was buried in Tucson. Mickey journeyed back to Tucson to find and view his mother's grave, then returned to Fort Whipple to enlist as a scout.

At this time Mickey Free was twenty years old, five foot seven, slender and at 125 pounds. He paid no attention to how he dressed, but usually wore a hat. He was secretive and withdrawn by nature, and was considered something of a man of mystery. He had already killed one white man, three Indians and five Mexicans, all but two with his deadly knife. Few people tried to associate with him because of his nature and his appearance with his cocked eye. Mickey Free, however, son of an Apache warrior and a Mexican girl, Apache captive during much of his youth and cause of a bitter war between Apaches and Americans, became one of the greatest scouts and interpreters in the army, trusted by his superiors including general officers with the most delicate assignments during the years of the Apache campaigns.

Chapter 4

Mutiny
on the Cibecue

The Apache Indians as a people separate from other Indians consisted of a number of nomadic tribes who spoke the same language, shared the same traits, and had a similar loose organization. The tribal leaders were chiefs, sub-chiefs, war chiefs and medicine men, some of the chiefs, such as Geronimo, also being medicine men. The tribal lands ranged from west Texas across the southern two-thirds of New Mexico, Arizona's southeast, and on into northern Old Mexico, the tribes usually being named for the regions they occupied.

General store at the Apache town of Cibecue on the Fort Apache Reservation in 1991.

The principal tribes are usually identified as the Mimbres Apaches who lived along the Mimbres River, the Mescalero Apaches near Tularosa, and the Warm Springs Apaches of Ojo Caliente in New Mexico, and in Arizona the Chiricahua Apaches of the Chiricahua and Dragoon Mountain ranges, the Arivaipa Apaches who lived along Arivaipa Creek, the Tonto Apaches

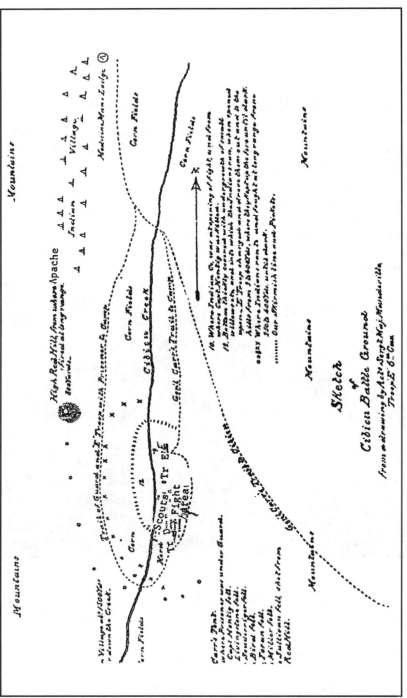

From "Cibicu Creek Fight in Arizona," H. B. Wharfield, Col., USAF Ret. Courtesy Arizona State Archives)

whose lands were in and around the basin of Tonto Creek, and the Coyotero or White Mountain Apaches who lived in the White Mountains and on lands ranging westward toward the Tonto Basin.

Integral to the Apache way of life was raiding other tribes, plundering, killing, and taking captives. The Spanish, Mexicans and Americans, when they arrived in territory which previously had been exclusively the Apaches', became their common enemy. Their ferocity, lack of any mercy, mutilations of the murdered and tortures of their adult captives made them universally hated and feared by all non-Apaches. Their name, Apache, comes from a Zuni word, "apachu," which means "enemy."

When there was no one else to fight, the Apaches fought among themselves. Animosities and fighting between bands and in the bands themselves were common. These animosities were some of the reasons the U.S. Army was able to recruit scouts from the Apache tribe and enlist them in the service. Apache scouts led army troops to even the most inaccessible Apache hideouts in the United States and Mexico, and fought side by side with the white soldiers against other Apaches. Army commanders freely acknowledged that the Apache scouts were crucial to the success of their campaigns.

The fact that the army was able to enlist so many Apaches as scouts is surprising in itself, but so is the fact that prominent Apaches were among those that enlisted. Some were chiefs, such as Chato (or Chatto), whose band the army pursued and captured and who then enlisted as a scout. Once enlisted, the scouts were generally faithful to the army's service. The one instance where some of them reverted to their tribal ties and turned against the soldiers was during an engagement at Cibecue Creek (sometimes spelled "Cibicu").

In 1871, President Ulysses S. Grant entertained a delegation of Indian chiefs and medicine men in Washington, D.C., and gave a commemorative medal to each one attending the council. Generally such visits to large cities had a devastating effect on the primitive Indians, who usually returned to their people urging the end of wars with the whites who had "as many people as there are leaves of grass," and whose superiority in

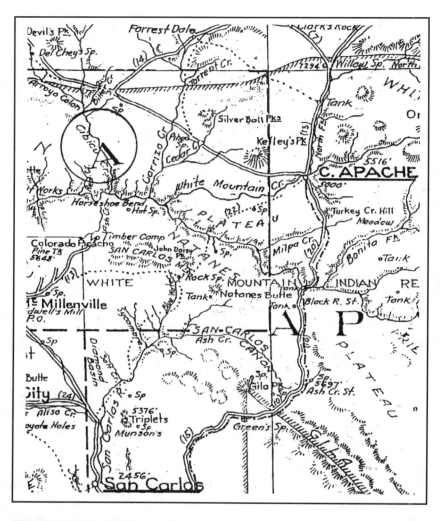

CIBECUE CREEK — FORT APACHE — SAN CARLOS AREA

from 1879 military map of Arizona

numbers, arms and supplies they realized made the Indians' victory an impossibility. One of the Indians on this occasion was an almost frail, introspective Coyotero Apache medicine man named Nock-ay-del-klinne.

For a time Nock-ay-del-klinne also attended a Christian school in Santa Fe, where he was exposed to the teachings of Christianity. He did not understand or accept it, but was influenced by some of what he learned, the resurrection of Christ and his fasting, praying and meditation. Upon his return to his own people, Nock-ay-del-klinne periodically withdrew into the mountains himself to fast, pray and meditate, and he became something of a mystic with increasing power and prestige among the Coyotero Apaches. By the spring of 1881, conditions were becoming serious on the White Mountain Apache Reservation and at its agency, Fort Apache, because of him.

In the previous year a census of the Apaches had been undertaken for the first time, part of a census of all Indians in the United States. On the White Mountain Reservation at the time were nine tribes of the Apaches, brooding over their restriction to the reservation territory and filled with hatred and suspicion toward other tribes and toward the white men who held them there, particularly the agents who cheated them outrageously when rations were issued. Near Fort Apache lived the Coyotero Apaches in small bands, each with a subchief who bore allegiance to the head chief, in this case Pedro, who lived on the White River north of the fort.

The census expedition into the White Mountains to count the disgruntled Apaches near Fort Apache left San Carlos, agency of the San Carlos Reservation to the south, in mid-February, 1881. Charles T. Connell was in charge, with J.C. Tiffany, Jr., son of the San Carlos agent as clerk, Mickey Free, interpreter, and Loco Jim, chief of the Indian scouts that included himself, Nal-zay, Skinney and Toggy-chewla. The census of the bands in the vicinity of San Carlos and its subagency at Fort Thomas had been taken, among them Apache chiefs Geronimo, Loco, Juh, Chihuahua, Chato and Natchez.

No other course was open to the census detail but to travel with a pack outfit, as every waterhole had to be visited to find the scattered bands. It was suspected that many would avoid the count because of their superstitious beliefs. At a camp some fifteen miles from Fort Apache, an Indian runner came into camp late one afternoon with news that a big fight had taken place between the Indians beyond the White River and that several had been killed. He reported that trouble was brewing between the bands and that the killings might set off a general uprising among the Apaches, who were in a state of unrest because of a medicine man who was inciting the Coyoteros, and others from a distance, with his prophecies and incantations.

The band of Pedro and Alchusay, both severely wounded in the fighting, was brought into Fort Apache, while the census takers worked on toward the fort, counting sullen Apaches and hearing complaints and secret whisperings about the medicine man. They arrived at Fort Apache in mid-February. Having learned of the increasing undercurrent of hostility toward whites, and that Indians of other branches of the Coyoteros were visiting the medicine man's camps for some secret purpose, an investigation was begun through Loco Jim, who had lived among the Coyoteros while the census was being taken. It was through him that the nature of the trouble brewing was first learned.

It was reported that the medicine man, Nock-ay-del-klinne, was going from camp to camp among the Apaches, telling them that in the fall he would raise from the dead all the Indians who had gone before, they would all meet in the Tonto Basin, and from there begin a war that would drive all the hated whites from the land. Fall was the time of year when the Indian agents issued passes to the Apaches to go hunting in the Tonto Basin. The medicine man had promised the followers of the fierce war chief Diablo that he would raise Diablo from the dead to lead them to glorious victory. Diablo had been killed six months previously by Alchusay, a war chief in Pedro's band. Bad blood already existed between the two, when at one of their meetings a quarrel during a gambling bout had broken out, resulting in the death of Diablo who was beloved by his clan as a fearless foe who hated the white men bitterly.

At every stop along the Cedar and Carizzo Creeks west of Fort Apache, the Indians held war dances in which the young warriors joined. Nock-ay-del-klinne admonished them at all times to repeat their war dances, so that their spirit would not flag, and to be ready to answer the call of the great war chief, Diablo. He promised that when the corn was ripe (September) he would go to the highest mountain, consult with the spirits, and return with the leader they worshiped. The medicine man took up residence on Cibecue Creek, forty-six miles west of Fort Apache, and there the neighboring Coyotero bands gathered for the "ghost dances" and to hear the medicine man's exhortations.

At the encampment on Cibecue Creek lived Pesh-e-magoon (meaning "Iron Tooth"), known as Sanchez, a war chief who was the successor to Diablo. The census party arrived there late in March. At other camps en route and while journeying there, Apaches were seen headed in both directions to and from the Cibecue. Scouts also reported that big dances were being held at Sanchez' camp. When the census party arrived there, however, it found only an ominous silence, Sanchez sullen, Nock-ay-del-klinne defiant, and resistant men with heads bowed,

Fort Apache, Arizona. This building, once the adjutant's office, is now the post office.

women and children out of sight in their wickiups.

Camped close to the Apache rancheria, the census takers made no effort to communicate with the Indians, later wrote Connell. "The presence of strangers did not interfere with the vehement exhortations of the scheming old medicine doctor," he said, "for around the roaring fires in their camp he directed the weird and ghostly dance. . . The flickering lights danced in unison with the crouched forms of the excited demons. The cracking embers of the roaring blaze cried out and mingled with the voices of the singing braves. Ever and anon, the passing of the wrinkled hags between the firelight and the dancing demons gave vivid thoughts of witches and voodoo hags of yore. No one dared approach, yet Loco Jim gained the information that pointed to serious results in the near future. These fantastic savages knew every ranch for hundreds of miles around, the strength of the garrison at Fort Apache, and the defenseless condition of San Carlos where no troops were stationed, except for the Indian scouts who were loyal."

At length Nock-ay-del-klinne condescended to talk if the white man (Connell) would come to his council. Fearing that refusal to listen to the medicine man would be misunderstood, the invitation was accepted though with regret. Shortly afterward, Connell found himself seated beside a blazing fire, apprehensively watching the movements of a hundred eager Coyoteros. With grand gestures, the medicine man stood in the center of the howling, painted dancers, taunting the lone white man with sneering jibes until rebuked by Sanchez.

Applauded by approving grunts, (listening Apaches would interject "Enjuh!" (Good!) if they approved of the speaker's words), the eloquent medicine man spoke as follows, directing his words to the white visitor: "Why should the paleface seek the haunts of the brave Coyoteros with their bad medicine? The belief of the Coyotero is different. There was only one brave among us, the Coyotero, who would keep the whites back: Diablo, the chieftain. His spirit hovers amid the rustling pine; the fluttering leaves denote his presence. The wail of the lion and the roar of the bear tell you that he is near. He will come again, not in spirit, but in the flesh to deliver us from the hated whites. Diablo guards our interest. Diablo seeks a remedy for our sorrows. Diablo will live again. In the dance we seek inspiration. With gliding, swaying movement we commune with the spirits. The dance inspires passion, faith, fury and strength. All this we will need at the resurrection of the great Diablo. Is it not I who receives the message at the resting place of the bones of Diablo?" and, indeed, it was to an Apache burial ground where Diablo had been interred that Nock-ay-del-klinne often withdrew to meditate.

Far into the night, the dancers retired. This method of inciting the once-peaceful Coyoteros had been going on for months, in the secrecy imposed by the medicine man. After a few hours the next day in the camp of Sanchez, counting as many people as they could despite the advice of Nock-ay-del-klinne, the census detail returned to San Carlos. The medicine man claimed the recording of names was "bad medicine," to have their names on paper made it easy for the devil to find them at any time, that they would not give the names of their women for the white men to locate and steal.

From the scouts, ample evidence of future trouble had been gained, and on the return to San Carlos a full report was made to the agent there, J. C. Tiffany, by Connell. It was communicated to the authorities, and steps were considered to counter the influence of the medicine man. Col. E. A. Carr, commander at Fort Apache, was also notified, as was the commander of the Department of Arizona, Gen. Orlando Willcox. Capt. Albert Sterling, chief of Indian scouts at San Carlos, was sent with a force of scouts to inquire more fully into the nature of the secret meetings and dances on the Cibecue, and on his return he reported that conditions were becoming very serious. The matter dragged along for several months, the correspondence delays working for disastrous results. Tiffany and Carr both, on separate occasions, invited the medicine man to come in and confer. Both times Nock-ay-del-klinne refused.

Very serious indeed was the worsening condition among the Apache scouts at Fort Apache. Lt. Tom Cruse, in charge of Indian scouts at the fort, sent one of his trusted subordinates to investigate, and the man returned with thoughts of resigning his post. Previously loyal scouts demanded passes to attend the dances and returned surly and uncooperative. When denied

Government housing at the Apache town of Cibecue on the Fort Apache reservation in 1991.

passes, they went to the dances anyway, and refused orders to return from others who were sent after them. Then Cruse himself attended one of the dances and what he saw surprised him. ". . . I was amazed at the fraternizing between tribes and elements which had always held for each other the most deadly aversion," he was to write later.

Early in August, 1881, an Indian inspector of the Interior Department who had considerable authority visited San Carlos. The state of affairs was explained to him, and at that time a suggestion was made that a telegram be sent to Gen. Carr in command at Fort Apache to the effect that Nock-ay-del-klinne should be arrested, or killed, or both. Carr had once again invited the medicine man to come in for a talk, and again he had refused. Carr sent a message to Tiffany saying that he was now fearful of an outbreak, that arresting the medicine man might precipitate war, and asking for Tiffany's views. It was then that Tiffany did send the telegram to Carr, saying that he wanted the medicine man arrested, or killed, or both. Carr telegraphed his assessment of the situation and his concerns to his departmental commander, Gen. Orlando Willcox, and on August 13th

Willcox telegraphed back his orders to Carr to arrest the medicine man, and bring him in as a prisoner.

Col. Carr, a graduate from West Point in 1850, was an officer with a long and distinguished record of service. He had won honors as an Indian fighter prior to the Civil War. In the Civil War he had won many honors for conspicuous gallantry as a field commander and was severely wounded in 1862. He moved to Arizona as a major with the Fifth Cavalry in 1872, from Fort McPherson, Nebraska, to Fort Lowell at Tucson, and now in 1881 was commanding troops of the Sixth Cavalry at Fort Apache.

Carr left Fort Apache on Monday, August 29, 1881, on his mission to arrest Nock-ay-del-klinne. He had with him about sixty-five men of Troops D and E of the Sixth Cavalry and a company of twenty-five Indian scouts. Troop D was commanded by Capt. Edmund W. Hentig, Troop E by Lt. William Stanton, and the scouts by Lt. Cruse. Others in the force were Lt. William Carter, adjutant, post surgeon McCreary, an interpreter named Hurley, boss packer Matt Noble, and Carr's fifteen-year-old son, on his summer vacation. The first day's march was about thirty miles, to a camp on Carizzo Creek.

Due to the uncertainties of the situation, the Indian scouts' guns and ammunition had been kept from them for some time, but at the camp Carr had a long talk with them concerning their mission to arrest the medicine man. He told them the man was not to be harmed, merely brought in for questioning about his activities, and he reminded them of their pledges to be loyal to the army and their commanders. Then he re-issued their ammunition to them, in readiness for any eventuality. One scout who knew the medicine man went on ahead to inform him why the troopers were coming; another who knew him remained with the armed column of scouts and troopers.

At about two the following afternoon Carr's command arrived at the Apache camp on Cibecue Creek and went directly to the lodge of Nock-ay-del-klinne. The soldiers formed a long line in front of the lodge, and Carr through the interpreter told the medicine man why they had come. The medicine man was arrested and put under the charge of Sgt. John McDonald and a guard detail. During this time an increasing crowd of Indians had gathered around, all plainly in a hostile mood. Everything had been done in the open, in full view and hearing of all the Indians crowding around. It was later charged that the interpreter was not sufficiently competent in the Indian language to make all of Carr's explanations and commands clear, but a few additional interpretations by the scouts for the moment eased the tensions among the onlooking Indians, which, it was very evident, was rapidly escalating.

Nock-ay-del-klinne was warned that he would be killed if he tried to escape, or if there was any resistance on the part of his followers. He said he understood, but that he wanted to finish eating. Most of the command then started back to Fort Apache, moving off down the creek to find a place to camp. Stanton's troopers and Cruse's scouts remained to escort the medicine man, who dallied but at length was told to come along. The troopers and scouts with his guard detail followed Troop D and the pack train which had gone on before. Carr later stated that he was unaware that his command was thus divided. From every direction, war-painted and heavily-armed Apaches had

Site of the Battle of Cibecue Creek on August 30, 1881. The soldiers camped at this spot on Cibecue Creek, where they were attacked by Apaches and mutinous scouts. Snipers fired into the camp from the top of the hill in the background.

been pouring into the Indian encampment, surrounding the medicine man and his escort, and adding to the apprehension of the commanding officers.

A couple of miles down Cibecue Creek, Carr had found a suitable place to stop for the night, and the column had begun its camping procedure. The men were setting it up, the pack train had been unloaded, the horses and mules sent out to herd. As the soldiers and scouts under Stanton and Cruse, with the medicine man in custody, arrived at the campsite, they were surrounded by hundreds of armed and frenzied Indians, who crowded in closer and closer to the camp. Carr told Capt. Hentig to keep them away, and Hentig did his best to clear them out, going about the camp telling the Indians to stay clear. Still, they continued to crowd in closer and closer to the camp.

Suddenly, the armed scouts, with loud war cries, began pumping shells into their rifles and firing at the troopers. One named Dead Shot was the first to fire; another named Dandy Jim was seen shooting Capt. Hentig in the back, through the heart. Hentig was dead immediately, as was his orderly, riddled with bullets. The troopers seized their weapons and poured out a withering return fire at the scouts and other Apaches who at once had joined in the assault on the army men. Scouts Dandy Jim and Skippy were seen trying to slip away with the medicine man, but some of the soldiers stopped them and were able to arrest and disarm a few of the mutinous scouts, while themselves making a hasty fortification of rocks and packs from the shelter of which they kept up their return fire. Some Indians rushed the herd, driving away about half of the command's horses and mules and killing the herder in the process.

During the melee, Nock-ay-del-klinne was killed trying to escape, and there are various stories about it. The most probable is that as he was crawling away, Sgt. McDonald and trumpeter William Benites both shot him, killing him instantly. Another is that a trumpeter named Ahrens shot him in the head, and he was left for dead. Later in the night, the sergeant of the guard, John A. Smith, observed the medicine man trying to crawl away, not yet dead though shot in the head. The sergeant, not wanting to start up more firing which by that time had ceased, grabbed an axe from the pack train equipment and dispatched the medicine man once and for all. Checking to be sure the man was dead, Smith noticed a shining object hanging on a beaded chain around his neck. Smith took it off, and found it to be the medal bestowed on the medicine man by

Store building at left and church buildings in right background at the Apache village at Cibecue in 1991.

then President Grant. One side of it showed a profile of Grant; the other bore the inscription, "On earth peace, good will towards men."

The battle which had begun at about five o'clock continued until dark, during which two more soldiers were killed and three wounded, two of whom later died. The Indians did not surround the soldiers' camp, but went into a camp of their own about five miles farther down Cibecue Creek. When night fell, a large excavation was made in Carr's tent, and all the dead in camp including the medicine man were buried in a mass grave. When everything had been put in order and the column reorganized, the return march to Fort Apache was begun under cover of darkness. Half of their mounts having been lost, the troopers alternated with others in walking and riding. It was a difficult trip, as the wounded were being transported as carefully as possible, and the Indians when the column was discovered kept up a constant harassment at every opportunity all the way in.

Carr's command reached Fort Apache once again about two-thirty that afternoon, to the immense relief of those remaining at the post. Word had reached the fort ahead of them that the entire force had been wiped out in the fight on Cibecue Creek. Cruse estimated that about eighteen Apaches had been killed by the soldiers. While the march back to Fort Apache was in progress the day after the fight, the Apaches discovered the mass grave at the campsite. In fury, frustration and vengeance, they dug up the bodies of the fallen soldiers, crushed their lifeless skulls with rocks, and horribly mutilated the bodies. The body of Nock-ay-del-klinne, the would-be savior who had met an ignominious death, was spirited away for an Apache burial.

The Indians went on a campaign of revenge for Nock-ay-del-klinne and their other dead. Travelers were waylaid and killed, ranches attacked, and even Fort Apache itself was briefly besieged. A few Indians sneaked onto the post, which was not actually a palisaded "fort" but a collection of buildings, and managed to set fire to some of the buildings. The fires were put out, the Apaches driven away, and the besiegers melted away into the night. Troopers continued to scout the broken hills of the reservation for roaming hostiles, with the aid of Sanchez and other chiefs who had surrendered. Coming again to the Cibecue battleground, they came upon the gruesome sight of the mutilated bodies of the soldiers, scattered on the ground, exposed to the skulking coyotes and vultures. The saddened soldiers re-buried the bodies, this time with full military honors, consumed with a vengeful fire themselves that boded ill for any hostile Apaches they were able to find.

At the first false news flash that the command had been wiped out in the battle on Cibecue Creek, sensationally headlined stories of the supposed annihilation had been carried on the front pages of newspapers around the world. General Willcox, the Arizona department commander, upon hearing the true report immediately rushed additional troops to the area, and the Indian resistance at once disappeared. Many of those sought for having participated in the uprising came in and surrendered. A few of the treacherous scouts came in, but most took to the wilderness and lived out their lives as hunted men.

Willcox, embarrassed at having this incident occur in the department he commanded, and not on the best of terms with Col. Carr anyway, preferred charges against Carr for neglect of duty, allowing his command to become separated and, therefore, endangering it, negligence at the campsite, and taking with him his armed scouts at a time when their loyalty was questionable. Carr demanded a court of inquiry to look into the charges. Most of his actions were vindicated except that he had allowed his command to become divided. While it happened without his knowledge, said the report, as commanding officer he should have known, and was responsible for it. The case was reviewed by President Chester A. Arthur himself who, dissatisfied with the state of the Department of Arizona, directed that Carr be admonished by the commanding general of the army. The directed admonishment to Carr was carried out.

The aftershocks of the battle on Cibecue Creek continued, however. Late in September, soldiers suddenly appeared at the camp of White Mountain Apaches living on the San Carlos Reservation. The soldiers were seeking Indians who had participated in the Cibecue Creek incident, but the thoroughly alarmed and frightened Indians ran to the camp of the Chiricahua Apaches for protection. This aroused the fierce and restless Chiricahuas, already chafing at reservation life and on September 30th about two hundred warriors led by their war chiefs, Geronimo, Juh and Natchez, broke out of the reservation headed for their traditional hideouts in the Sierra Madre Mountains of Old Mexico, raiding, plundering and killing in southeastern Arizona as they went.

At Cedar Springs, fifteen miles from the sub-agency at Fort Thomas, the hostile Chiricahuas on October 3rd attacked Samaniego's freight wagon train, killing five teamsters and Bartolo Samaniego, brother of the owner of the train. They also attacked and killed four linemen working as a repair crew on the military telegraph line between Forts Thomas and Grant. Troopers following the Indians came upon this attack scene, and while they were examining the bodies, they were fired upon by the Indians from ambush. The troopers returned the fire, which continued until dark. Then, under cover of the night, the Apaches withdrew to continue their flight to Old Mexico (see chapter on Cottonwood Canyon).

Charges of mutiny, desertion, and murder were brought on November 11, 1881, against five of the scouts who had mutinied at the battle on Cibecue Creek. Two were dishonorably discharged and sentenced to long terms at the army prison on Alcatraz Island. Sergeant Dead Shot, Sergeant Dandy Jim and Private Skippy were sentenced to be hanged. At Fort Grant, Arizona, on March 12, 1882, at 12:30 p.m., before the entire garrison dressed in full uniform and standing at attention, the three treacherous scouts were brought to the gallows and hanged as their sentences directed.

Returnees to the scenes of historic events in Arizona's Old West can visit the present-day Apache village of Cibecue and the area where the battle between the Indians and troopers occurred. U.S. Highway 60 crosses the Apache reservations from Globe to Showlow, and on the way descends into the canyon of the Salt River. Approximately thirty miles north of the Salt River bridge, the well-marked road to Cibecue turns off the highway to the north. The road, paved all the way, traverses some of the most scenic country to be found anywhere—between mountain ridges and mesas covered with pines and juniper, red cliffs and hills contrasting with the green of the vegetation, the little creeks in the arroyos sometimes flowing.

After about twelve miles, the road comes to a broad, scenic valley some two or three miles long through which Cibecue Creek flows from north to south. At the upper end of the valley, across the creek, is the present Cibecue village. The wickiups have been replaced by government housing. There are also a sawmill, a modern medical clinic, a general store, several churches and a small shopping center.

A bridge crosses Cibecue Creek at the village, the bridge being within the area of the troops' encampment. The main portion of the encampment was just downstream from the present bridge, east of and below the sawmill that is on the west side. A high red bluff stands just north of the road at the west end of the bridge; from the top of this bluff Apache snipers fired into the troopers' camp during the battle. Time has erased all traces of the campsite or the battle, though some shell casings and other small evidences have been recovered. The camp of Nock-ay-del-klinne and Sanchez was a couple of miles upstream, in an open area on the west bank. There is no monument at the campsite or battleground.

A monument is found at Fort Apache itself, the remains of which still exist, as it was turned over to the Apaches when the wars were over and it was no longer needed. About eight miles north of the Cibecue Junction on Highway 60 is the turnoff to the east from the highway to Fort Apache about twenty-three miles away on Arizona 73. Sad to say, the old fort is deteriorating with age and lack of maintenance. Some of the original buildings still stand, among which is the log building that was the headquarters of General George Crook when he commanded the military there. Near this log building is the monument commemorating the battle at Cibecue Creek.

Chapter 5

The Affair at Cottonwood Canyon

It was May 8, 1889, when the west-bound Southern Pacific train stopped at the dusty, desolate little railroad town named Willcox, in southern Arizona territory, some sixty miles west of the New Mexico border. It was met by army Major Joseph Washington Wham, a paymaster, and a heavily-armed escort of soldiers. From the express car they took a heavy oak chest, filled with bags of gold and silver coins, pay for the troopers at four army posts in the territory and totaling some $45,000. The paymaster and his escort, riding in two mule-drawn army vehicles, set out for Major Wham's station thirty miles north of Willcox. Fort Grant, on the southwest slope of Mount Graham, would be the first at which pay would be distributed to the soldiers, who were paid three times a year.

Fort Grant in 1881. From this post, Paymaster Wham set out for Fort Thomas. The payroll holdup occurred en route. (Arizona Historic Photos)

Seven miles south of the fort they passed near the Sierra Bonita Ranch of the prominent rancher Henry Hooker, who contracted to supply beef to a number of army posts. At the ranch Hooker often entertained the officers of Fort Grant and their ladies. A little farther on, a couple of miles from the fort, the paymaster's party passed through a settlement called Bonita, where the enlisted men found entertainment. It was typical of ramshackle towns that existed just outside all army

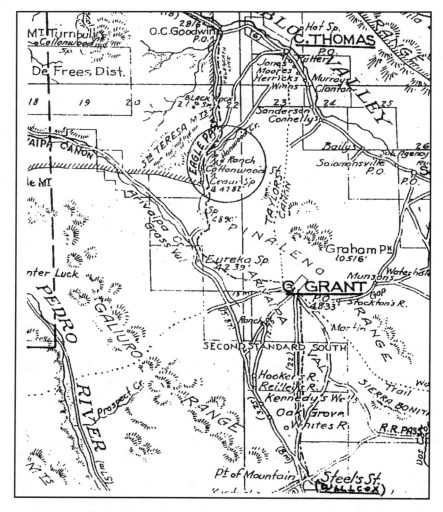

FORT GRANT — COTTONWOOD CANYON
FORT THOMAS AREA

from 1879 military map of Arizona

posts then. It consisted mostly of saloons, gambling dens, dance halls, bawdy houses, and a few stores, inhabited by whiskey-sellers, card sharks, red-light girls and other army hangers-on, with some enlisted men's families, storekeepers, merchants and cowpokes.

Such places as Bonita were called "hog farms," because on paydays they were overrun by sellers of rot-gut whiskey brought in by the hogshead, by swarms of itinerant gamblers, prostitutes flocking from Willcox and other small towns, all intent on separating the soldiers from their pay. The towns also attracted outlaws and other frontier characters of unsavory reputation. One of the most notorious of them all had killed his first man in Bonita on August 17, 1877. Seventeen-year-old Henry Antrim, who worked at a hay camp for a contractor furnishing hay to the fort, got into a quarrel over a card game that day in Adkins' dance hall. His antagonist was blacksmith Frank P. Cahill, called "Windy" because of his domineering, overbearing manner. He got his kicks from tormenting the boy, and after they had exchanged a few obscene epithets a wrestling match ensued. The much-heavier and older Cahill had the boy down, when Antrim grabbed Cahill's gun and shot him through the stomach. Cahill died the next day. Antrim fled to New Mexico, hid out at a ranch for a while, and emerged with a new name. It was William Bonney, alias "Billy the Kid."

Old building at present-day Bonita dates to 1882 and is not the place where the young "Billy the Kid" killed a man in 1877.

Having paid Fort Grant's soldiers some $15,000, Major Wham took the road to other army posts. A closer look at him is in order, as he was the central figure in the chain of events to follow. He was not a favorite among the soldiers; he was authoritarian, stubborn and suspected of lacking in nerve. That was despite the fact that he had served through the Civil War as an enlisted man, though discharged in 1865 as a first lieutenant. In 1867 he rejoined the army as a second lieutenant, but was released again in 1871. In 1877, he had been re-commissioned from civil life as a major and paymaster. The reminiscences of a man who drove teams for him in Wyoming and Arizona illustrates the soldiers' reasons for disliking Major Wham.

"Major Wham and I never did get along," wrote James B. Glover. "He was a _____ on animals, and you know how an old packer and driver likes to take care of his animals. Wham was always late starting, and then he was in a hurry to get to his destination and would take it out on his animals. Once we had given our animals a hard ride and had come to water. I wanted to stop and rest the mules before giving them a drink but he wanted to go on. I said we had gone far enough but he insisted. So I gave the mules a little water but not much—they were too warm. He wanted me to give them more. I said, 'No, if I give these mules more they will die.' He answered, 'I am in charge; do as I say.' I replied, 'All right.'

"Well, we went about a mile and one mule dropped dead. A few miles farther, and another dropped. I was mad and said so. He ordered me to get down off the box. I kicked my bedroll off, then climbed down myself. He said, 'Leave that whip.' I said, 'No, that whip is my private property.' 'Well,' he swore, 'leave it anyway.' I was sitting on my blankets with the whip in my hand and I pulled my pistol. Wham was a natural coward—I have seen him dry many times—so he gathered up the reins and with but two mules drove on, without me.

"I waited for the stage and rode back to San Carlos (head-quarters of the Apache Indian agency). When Wham arrived after his trip he saw me working round the post and went to the quartermaster with a complaint about me. As a result, I told my story, and Wham was made to pay for the mules and to pay my fare on the stage. For about two years he was on half pay while the rest of his salary went to settling up just such things as this."

The next post on Wham's itinerary after Fort Grant was Fort Thomas, forty-five miles northerly by the military road around the west end of Mount Graham, then winding through broken terrain down to the desert. The soldiers at both Fort Grant and Fort Thomas were black enlisted men with white officers. Wham set out on the morning of May 11, 1889, in an army "dougherty wagon" ambulance with his clerk, W. J. Gibbon, a white man, beside him. On the driver's seat in front of them were a black teamster, Private Caldwell, driving, and Sergeant Benjamin Brown, in charge of the escorting soldiers, all of the 24th infantry. Under their feet in the "boot" of the ambulance was the oaken pay chest containing sacks of $20, $10 and $5 gold coins, and sacks of silver change. The total of its contents was $28,345.10.

Behind them in the escort wagon rode the men, Corporal Isaiah Mays, and Privates George Arrington, Benjamin Burge, Oscar Fox, Thornton Ham, Julius Harrison, George Short, James Wheeler, Squire Williams and James Young. This wagon was specially arranged with seats for five soldiers on each side of the wagon, facing each other, so that they commanded a good view of the opposite sides of the road. The driver was another black teamster, Private Hamilton.

By mid-day the caravan arrived at Cedar Springs station, also the headquarters of the Barney Norton ranch. Here the traveling party was fed, and the teams were changed, twelve mules having been brought out from Fort Grant the previous day as relief. While they were there, another traveler on the military road that day came in. It was a young black woman named Frankie Campbell, going from Bonita to the settlement outside the gates of Fort Thomas known as Maxi. Though married, Frankie was a lady of easy virtue who also engaged in loan-sharking, lending money between paydays to enlisted men at usurious rates. Frankie wanted to arrive at Maxi before the troopers at Fort Thomas were paid to settle some of those accounts owed her. She had left Bonita at sun-up, stopped along the road at "Shotgun" Smith's for a cup of coffee and at "Sam's water station" to talk to him and a Mexican. For some reason, the Mexican warned her several times not to try to go through to Fort Thomas that day, as her life might be in danger.

The paymaster's procession left Cedar Springs before Frankie, but she soon overtook it. That was at the top of a steep grade that descended into Cottonwood Canyon. In the canyon the road narrowed as it ran through a gorge with steep banks on both sides before ascending again. Frankie passed the wagons and rode on ahead. Just as she cleared the narrowest spot, a sudden noise behind her spooked her horse. It jumped, throwing Frankie to the ground. Looking around, she found the noise had been made by a huge boulder falling squarely in the middle of the road between her and the paymaster's vehicles.

Road from Fort Grant to Fort Thomas at Cottonwood Canyon. Boulder rolled into narrow road at right, halted the paymaster's wagon and was the scene of the robbery.

The ambulance and escort wagon stopped short of the boulder blocking the road. All of the soldiers in the escort wagon were called up to shove the boulder aside, and Private Harrison on reaching it said, "Boys, that rock was rolled there by hands." Just then there were shouts from the rocky precipice above the road. "Git away from there; git movin', you _____ scala-wags!" ordered a man's voice. Looking up, the soldiers saw a number of men along the ridge with rifles, and bullets began to spatter down. The soldiers ran for their guns, but they were hopelessly caught in the fire raining down on them from men concealed in rifle pits they had constructed along the brow of the rocky ridges.

What happened then was a confused and bloody tangle that never was completely sorted out. Harrison's ear lobe was clipped by a bullet. Sergeant Brown was shot through the stomach and fell. Private Young ran to him, picked him up, and carried him out of the line of fire. In doing so, Young's belt buckle was struck by a bullet that was deflected to tear three cartridges out of his belt, but he was not wounded. At the rock, Frankie Campbell threw her shawl over Private Fox and told him to stay down and he would be all right. Then she dived behind a bush to watch the rest of the action. Corporal Mays, a bullet in his shoulder, ran away toward the rear and down the gorge.

Rocks piled on hillside to form rifle pits above the Fort Grant-Fort Thomas road, sheltered the robbers of the army payroll.

Major Wham had been leaning out of the ambulance, just at the point of telling the driver he thought they could go around the rock in the road, when the shooting began. He jumped out and dived behind some boulders, followed by Gibbon. Neither was wounded, though bullets passed through Gibbon's sleeve and hat. The troopers tried to make a fight of it, but gradually began to sustain wounds from the crossfire of the rifle pits above. Burge, Thornton, Ham, Wheeler, Arrington, Williams, and teamster Hamilton all were wounded in the arms or legs. Leaderless, they began to run from the battle scene. Wham called on Mays to stop running and come back, but he kept on going, followed by the rest of the men.

One of the men in the rifle pits above half rose, and motioned to Wham to move away. Wham then ran after his men, saying later that he did so to rally them for a fight. The soldiers, most of them wounded, stayed down the gorge out of rifle range. Then some of the riflemen descended into the road, took the paymaster's oak chest out of the ambulance, and broke it open with an axe. Major Wham could not actually see this taking place, but could hear the blows of the axe on the wooden chest. The highwaymen emptied the contents of the box into gunny sacks, cut the mules out of their harness and drove them away from the scene, climbed back up the walls of the gorge, mounted their horses and fled. The box was left in the road, along with three dead mules killed during the exchange of bullets, which lasted half an hour.

Someone had heard the firing and notified Barney Norton, who arrived too late with a bunch of his cowboys. Norton sent a messenger to Fort Thomas, fifteen miles away, and the post commander sent back a surgeon and wagons to transport the wounded. The cowboys rounded up some of the scattered mules and hitched them to the ambulance, which started toward Fort Thomas carrying the most seriously wounded. Investigators who rushed to the scene found nine rude rifle pits on the brow of the gorge, made by piling up the native rocks. From some of them, sticks had been pointed down to the road below, to give the impression that they were rifle barrels aiming downward.

When the news of the audacious robbery broke, it caused a tremendous sensation. "In a few days," reported the *Arizona Citizen* of Tucson on September 26, 1889, "the whole country swarmed with soldiers, detectives, and deputy marshals. Scouting parties were sent from Forts Lowell, Huachuca, Bowie, Grant, Thomas and Bayard in New Mexico, and San Carlos. They were unable to find the trail owing to the fact that the whole country surrounding the place where the robbery occurred had been cut to pieces by scouting soldiers, before the trackers were taken to the place." Because of this, the highwaymen made a clean getaway.

The authorities were not without suspects, however. Major Wham and the men of his escort thought they recognized some of the robbers, whom they saw rising up from their breastworks to shoot or running between the rifle pits. Frankie Campbell thought she knew some of them, too. Reports began to trickle in of civilians in the little towns along the Gila River and farmers in the regions around them acting suspiciously, or suddenly and mysteriously coming into possession of uncharacteristic amounts of money. Many of them were of the highly moralistic Mormon faith. A $500 reward was offered by United States Marshal W. K. Meade for the arrest of each of the robbers. Deputy sheriff W. K. Parks of Graham County concentrated on the crime, gathering evidence and sifting clues, and a number of suspects were soon in custody.

The first arrested was Frankie Campbell, who seemed to know and tell a lot about the event she had witnessed from behind the bush. It became apparent that she had no complicity in the robbery and she was released, eventually to become a witness for the prosecution. The next arrested was a border character named William Ellison Beck, popularly known as "Cyclone Bill." Bill was long-winded, a tin-horn gambler and con man. A gunshot wound had crippled one of his legs, which was much shorter than the other, and he walked with a distinctive limp. One of the soldiers was sure he recognized that limp in a man going from one rifle pit to another, so Bill was arrested.

For a time Bill basked in the notoriety that attended persons with enough nerve to accomplish such a successful coup, but at length produced an alibi. The *Arizona Citizen* on June 6, 1889, reported that "Mr. and Mrs. Tidwell of Eagle Creek, 85 miles from the scene of the robbery, swore positively that 'Cyclone' came to their home on Friday, May 10th, and remained there until the forenoon of May 12th, and went from there to Morenci. . . On this testimony the defendant was discharged. . ."

In time seven men were arrested and charged with the

robbery. They were M. E. Cunningham, Gilbert Webb, Warren Follett, Lyman Follett, Ed Follett, Thomas Lamb and David Rogers. All were Mormons except Cunningham. At his hearing before the U. S. Commissioner, Ed Follett was discharged and the rest held in jail. Bail was set at $10,000 each but only Gilbert Webb made bail and the others continued to languish in durance vile. The *Arizona Citizen* stated on September 28, 1889, that the grand jury had handed down indictments against all the seven men charged.

For a time the in-fighting between political enemies, antagonistic parties, and attorneys for the prosecution and defense took center stage. No more colorful cast of characters was ever assembled, nor any occasion when political heavyweights slugged it out on the front pages of the newspapers, ever took place in Arizona territorial history, with the possible exception of the Earp saga in Tombstone. U. S. Marshal W. K. Meade and the district judge, W. H. Barnes, were bitter political enemies, holdover appointees of an outgoing administration, whose successors had not yet been named. Barnes was friendly with one of the men accused in the case, and unknown to others involved in it had arranged with Judge Hawkins of Prescott to replace him at the trial.

It was also unknown to the grand jury, which feared that Barnes' rancor might intimidate witnesses. The jurors became alarmed at a remark made by Barnes when the sufficiency of Webb's bailers was questioned. "So far as the sufficiency of the sureties is concerned, I deem it ample," he snapped. "The bond is valid and binding and I know one of the signers upon it who is a surety upon a bond of the U. S. marshal for two or three times the amount." The aroused grand jury then sent a telegram to the Attorney General in Washington complaining of Barnes' conduct and requesting that another judge be assigned to the case. Barnes got hold of a copy of the telegram. He called the grand jury into session, castigated them as a bunch of "character assassins," and summarily dismissed them as "'unworthy to sit in any court of justice."

A young, relatively unknown Pima County district attorney, Richard E. Sloan, was then appointed a justice of the territorial Supreme Court and assigned to be the presiding judge at the Wham trial. It would be Sloan's first major case in a career that saw him rise to be governor of Arizona. The government's prosecutor would be District Attorney Harry R. Jeffords assisted by attorneys Selim M. Franklin of Tucson and Col. William Herring of Tombstone, where he once was Wyatt Earp's lawyer. For the defense it was Marcus Aurelius (Mark) Smith, brilliant young attorney from Tombstone, and Ben Goodrich, then practicing in Phoenix. Smith and Goodrich had been law partners in Tombstone, having arrived there on the same stagecoach, and where Goodrich had represented the widely-notorious outlaw John Ringo. Smith would become the territorial delegate to Congress and a U. S. senator. They were assisted by the law firm of Hereford and Hereford.

Sometime after his release on bond, the only one of the robbery suspects to make bail, Gilbert Webb, was for some reason re-arrested and jailed in Prescott. Naturally, his protests were loud and long, and soon he was freed again. He later claimed that, at this time, he had been given $400 in gold coins in compensation for the time he spent in the Prescott jail. Then he made the mistake of turning up in a Tucson gambling house and wagering some gold coins. The suspicious proprietors reported this to the authorities and Webb was picked up again. He was not held, but about $1,000 in gold coins he had left at a hotel deposit box was seized to be held as evidence.

On November 11, 1889, exactly six months after the robbery, the trial of the seven defendants finally opened. District Attorney Jeffords stated that the government preferred to prosecute them jointly, rather than separately. Defense counsel Mark Smith made two motions to dismiss the case, which were denied. The indictments were read and the taking of testimony began. Major Wham began testifying on November 15th, giving his story of what had taken place during the robbery and claiming that he had run from the battle scene to rally his men. He identified Gilbert Webb, Warren Follett and David Rogers as some of the holdup men he recognized. A quantity of $20 gold pieces were spread out on a table as an exhibit, and Wham stated that he was positive that they were coins taken in the robbery.

The court then took a lunch break, during which defense

attorney Mark Smith went to the bank. He had a quantity of his personal funds changed into $20 gold pieces, and returned to the courtroom with them in his pocket. When he began his cross-examination of Wham, he asked if the witness was positive the gold coins on exhibit were part of the robbery loot. Wham said he was. Smith took a handful of the gold coins from his pocket, dumped them on the table, mixed them with those already there, and asked Wham to pick out those he had identified as part of the loot. Wham sheepishly had to admit he could not, and away went a lot of his credibility.

Soldiers testifying were Sergeant Brown, Corporal Mays, and Privates Short, Arrington, Young, Burge and Harrison. All told their versions of the fight, and of falling back because of wounds. They identified all of the defendants except Thomas Lamb as men they saw firing from the precipice or running between the rifle pits. All used the phrase "to the best of my acknowledge and belief," which seemed to raise the increasing level of merriment among the spectators with each repetition. The soldiers said they had seen the defendants on occasion at Fort Grant and Bonita, but all were local residents who had occasion to do business there.

Frankie Campbell's testimony for the prosecution was a source of comic relief to the onlookers, as she was unimpressed by the solemnity of the proceedings and by turns was coy, pert, tart-tongued and outspoken. She said she knew Private Caldwell, one of the teamsters, and that she last saw him running in the direction of Fort Thomas so fast he got there before she did. She was the first witness to identify Thomas Lamb as one of the riflemen. Asked whether she saw Major Wham, she said the last she saw of him he was running away so fast "you could play checkers on his coat-tails." When one of the lawyers objected to a question and the judge upheld the objection, Frankie brought down the house by inquiring, "Who's boss around here, the judge, jury or lawyers?" During her entire testimony, too, she had airily waved her right hand about. Asked why she did so, she replied, "Well, my left hand wasn't sworn in."

The trial dragged on for more than a month, with more than 165 testifying, most of them for the defense. All of the defendants took the stand to swear they had no knowledge of the robbery and were miles from its scene when it happened. Most people in the little towns and on farms along the Gila River, from which the accused came, were members of the closely-knit Mormon community that had little sympathy for the government and were stonily opposed to the trial. One farmer testified for the prosecution that he saw one of the defendants hide something in the farmer's haystack and come back later to get it. The man had given him $25 to burn some sacks of the kind that held the payroll money. He admitted that, after giving this testimony at a preliminary hearing, he had tried to have it stricken from the record. His neighbors, having heard of it, had done their work on him.

After thirty-three days, the trial ended. For two more days the attorneys thundered and soared in flights of spell-binding oratory during the closing arguments, and on Saturday morning, December 14th, Judge Sloan gave his charge to the jury. At noon it began its deliberations and was out for two hours most of which time was occupied by eating lunch. The jury foreman, Heil Hale, read the verdict: "We, the jury, find the defendants not guilty," and it was all over. Some of the jurors said later that they thought some of the defendants were guilty, but since they had been tried jointly felt that if some were innocent, all should be found not guilty. This reasoning was refuted in the judge's charge. It clearly said, "If, however, upon all the evidence in the case, the jury is satisfied that certain defendants are guilty as charged in the indictment and that others of the defendants are not guilty, it should say so in the verdict. The jury has the power to say that any or all of the defendants are guilty, or that any or all of the defendants are not guilty."

Public sentiment over the trial's outcome was expressed in an editorial in the *Arizona Citizen* on December 16, 1889. It said in part: "We find, however, deep seated dissatisfaction among our best citizens over the verdict given, partly because of the undue haste with which the report was made, and partly for the reason that it was evident, even to the most unobserving, that the great mass of testimony offered by the government could not in one short hour have been given the consideration it deserved... A trial that occupied the attention of the court for a full month was not in the eyes of the thinking public to be thus lightly disposed of, and the sentiments of the people are loudly outspoken against it. To still further heighten public opinion in the matter is the reports that some of the accused had not been free a half hour before they were threatening to kill some of the witnesses who had testified against them with bullets in case they returned to their homes in Graham County. . ."

For all practical purposes, however, the affair at Cotton-wood Canyon was at an end. No one was ever again arrested or charged in the robbery. The identity of the highwaymen and what became of their loot has never been discovered. If some or all of the defendants were, in fact, the guilty parties, they would have had to use all of their booty for the costs of the trial, for attorneys' fees and the cost of transporting, housing and feeding the huge wave of witnesses. Under military law, Major Wham himself remained liable for the entire amount stolen until he was relieved of it by a special act of Congress on January 21, 1891. Wham retired from the service in May, 1901, and died in Washington, D. C. on December 21, 1908, at the age of 68.

Cedar Springs, the station on the old military road between Forts Grant and Thomas near which Major Wham's party was robbed was also the scene of an earlier and equally famous incident in Arizona history. It is only a few miles from the San Carlos Indian Reservation. Early in October, 1881, the restless and warlike Chiricahua Apaches broke out of the reservation, bound for their traditional hideouts in the Sierra Madre mountains of Old Mexico. Led by war chiefs Geronimo and Natchez, about 75 to 100 warriors attacked the freight wagon train of the Samaniego brothers at about eight o'clock on the morning of October 3rd. This was at a point said to be about a mile east of Cedar Springs. The men in the wagon train, unaware that the Apaches had fled the reservation and outnumbered more than ten to one, put up a terrific fight before Bartolo Samaniego and five teamsters were killed. The Indians shot six mules, slit open sacks and dumped out the flour, and rifled the freight wagons.

A short distance west of Cedar Springs the Apaches came upon a telegraph operator and four linemen engaged in repairing the military telegraph line that ran alongside the road. The Apaches butchered them also. Captain George B. Sanford and his cavalrymen pursuing the hostile warriors came upon the scene and were examining the bodies when they were fired upon from ambush by the Apaches. This fight began about three in the afternoon and continued until darkness fell, when the Apaches fled and escaped under the cover of the night. Then they split up into several bands, raiding and plundering as they went, crossing the border into the mountains of Mexico.

Fort Grant and Fort Thomas still exist today as Arizona communities though given up as military posts long ago. You can still drive part of the old military road between them, with the aid of a four-wheel drive vehicle, since they have not been maintained for many years. The scenes of these famous events in Arizona Territory are more easily reached by a modern, well-maintained dirt road, which leaves Fort Grant and Bonita westerly. After a scenic drive along Arivaipa Creek for some twenty-five miles, just after entering Arivaipa Canyon, one comes to a sign pointing the way over the mountain pass toward the Gila River, and the towns along it and U. S. 70.

Turning right there, after about six or seven miles one comes to a sign pointing out the road to Cedar Springs, four miles to the east, and now merely a camp. Past this sign on the main road a couple of miles is the descent into the gorge of Cottonwood Canyon. At almost the bottom of the wash, at its narrowest point, the boulder was rolled down from the rocky hillside to block the road, which is wider now, not the rutted, one-track trail it was then. On the rocky hillsides right and left, the riflemen lay in wait, those many years ago, for the paymaster's treasure.

Chapter 6

Arizona Characters

Arizona Territory seemed to have more than its share of people with traits of personality beyond the ordinary, even exceeding those we refer to off-handedly as "he's a character." Not only did the open and free lifestyle of the frontier attract such people, others were driven to it when their peculiarities were found unacceptable elsewhere. Whether their characteristics leaned toward the tragic or the comedic, or a combination of both, the stories handed down about them are fascinating sidelights of territorial life.

One of these mentioned several times in chronicles of Arizona was Jerry Barton, a very large citizen of enormous strength. Primarily, in Arizona, he was a saloonkeeper, but in legend he was a brawler and fighter who killed more than one man with his bare fists. Jerry was also adept with a six-gun when the occasion demanded, as his scores in desperate shoot-outs attest. Yet with all that, there was a gentler side to Jerry Barton that showed through on occasion. For all his forcefulness, he was a family man, and in his speech stuttered badly. Born in New York in 1849, he grew up in Tennessee. When he killed a man there, he fled to the Arizona desert, where it was considered impolite, even dangerous, to inquire of a man about his background if he didn't volunteer the information.

Jerry surfaced in Phoenix, tending bar in Kellum's Saloon where, said the *Arizona Miner* newspaper of Prescott in August 6, 1876, a drunk named Henry King called Barton some choice names. Incensed, Barton invited him to repeat them outside. He did, and a fight ensued. King took some blows to the head, and was knocked down unconscious in the street. In a few minutes, he was dead. Barton was arrested, but the charges against him were dismissed at a hearing the next day. For about a year beginning early in 1878 he was part owner of a couple of saloons in Globe where, it was reported, he gave another man a fearful beating.

In 1879 the fabulous silver camp known as Tombstone was

growing in southern Arizona, along with a satellite town called Charleston on the bank of the San Pedro River, nine miles to the west. Barton became a partner in a Charleston saloon in 1880, where on October 10th he shot and killed a man. The October 12, 1880, edition of the Tombstone *Epitaph* said: "Our sister town of Charleston was the scene of a shooting affray on Sunday night last, about 10 o'clock, which resulted in the killing of a man named Merrill, by Barton, of the saloon firm of Barton and Sperry.

". . . Merrill was somewhat under the influence of liquor and with three companions had been taking in (shooting up) the town, discharging their pistols in the streets and in the saloons. During the racket Merrill asked Barton for some money with which to gamble. Barton refused him and Merrill went off, threatening vengeance. Fearing trouble, Barton went off and did not return for about two hours. Shortly after Barton made his re-entry, Merrill came into the saloon and fired a shot at Barton, missing him. Barton returned the fire, shooting in all three shots, the result being the killing outright of Merrill. A coroner's inquest was begun yesterday morning and continued until today at 10 a.m. . . Public sympathy seems to be almost entirely with Barton."

The October 14th *Epitaph* reported: "The examination of Jerry Barton, on the charge of murder, in killing Merrill at Charleston on Sunday last, was concluded before Justice Burnett on Wednesday night, and resulted in the prisoner being held to appear before the next grand jury on the charge of murder. The judge . . . said he had no doubt the grand jury would exonerate Barton but thought it better that the prisoner go before it. He fixed bail at $2,500 which was promptly furnished by Frank Stilwell and John Campbell. From what we can learn, the sympathy of almost the entire community is with Barton." Eventually, this charge against Barton was also dismissed.

The above article has significance because of the other people mentioned in it, two of whom came to violent deaths. Justice Burnett was the legendary Charleston justice of the peace Jim Burnett, who declared himself independent of the Pima County legal system and took his compensation by simply pocketing the fines he levied. After his days as a judge, Burnett took up ranching, and was accused by cattle baron William Greene of blowing up a dam on the San Pedro River resulting in the drowning of Greene's little daughter. Encountering Burnett on Tombstone's Allen Street in front of the O. K. Corral, Greene shot Burnett dead on the spot. Frank Stilwell was a deputy sheriff for Charleston to the famous Sheriff Johnny Behan of Tombstone during the Earp years. Stilwell turned to outlawry, and it was he who assassinated Wyatt Earp's brother, Morgan, by shooting him in the back from a dark alley as Morgan was playing pool in the rear of Hatch's Saloon in Tombstone. Stilwell himself was run down and killed by Wyatt Earp and Doc Holliday in the Tucson railroad yard.

Almost a year to the day from the time he killed Merrill, Barton was in hot water again for shooting a Mexican. The *Epitaph* on October 11, 1881, reported: "About eight o'clock on Sunday morning last, Jerry Barton, who keeps a saloon in Charleston, shot a Mexican named Jesus Gamboa, inflicting an ugly though not necessarily fatal wound. From the Mexican, who was brought to the hospital here today, an *Epitaph* reporter learned the following . . : Jesus and several friends of his had been carousing and drinking around for several days,

Bare adobe walls and mesquite in the ghost town of Charleston on the San Pedro River where Jerry Barton kept a saloon.

spending between them about $40 in Barton's saloon. . . The party, having spent nearly all their money, broke up, each going his own way.

"Jesus went into Jerry's saloon and sat down, when the proprietor came up to him and said, 'You can't have anything to drink here.' . . . Jesus made no resistance but laid his head on his arms which rested on the table." Barton then struck the Mexican on the head with a pistol, which discharged. The bullet struck Gamboa's left shoulder, coursed under the skin across his back, and lodged near the right shoulder blade. Barton was arrested, but released under bond of $700. Apparently he felt it to be the proper time for a little vacation, for according to the memoirs of another of Sheriff Behan's deputies, Billy Breakenridge, Barton jumped bail and went to Tucson, where he was arrested and returned to the Tombstone pokey of the new Cochise County.

According to the memoirs of Billy Breakenridge, Barton while being held there came to the aid of a jailer during a successful jail break. Barton was being held with three other prisoners, Milt Hicks for rustling, Yank Thompson for horse thievery, and Jim Sharpe for murder. When an assistant jailer named Mason attempted to allow a trusty into the cell to remove some slops, Hicks caught Mason by the arm. As the two were wrestling, Thompson and Sharpe ran outside, and as Hicks broke away he tried to close the jail door. Mason, however, got his shoulder between the door and the jamb. The prisoners would have broken Mason's arm had not Jerry Barton come to his aid, but even Barton's great strength could not prevent the prisoners from jamming the door shut, locking it, and making good their escape.

Jesus Gamboa, the Mexican that Barton had shot, eventually returned to Old Mexico and again the charge against Jerry was dropped. According to Breakenridge's memoirs, when once asked why he shot so many men, Barton replied, "M-m-my t-t-trigger fi-finger stu-stu-stutters." And another time, when asked how many men he had killed, Barton thought for a moment, then asked, "D-d-do y-y-you c-c-count M-M-Mexicans?"

Jake Swart also ran a saloon in Charleston, and though

they were competitors and Jake was a Democrat while Barton was a Republican, they were socially friendly. At one time during a political campaign, Mark Smith, destined for fame in Arizona history but then an attorney in Tombstone, was running for his first term for district attorney as a Democrat. A Republican candidate for the state legislature was General Wardell, and they chose the same night to make political speeches in Charleston. Jake Swart collected all the old barrels and boxes he could find, to build a bonfire in front of his place to attract the crowd. Barton, not to be outdone, hired some Mexican woodchoppers to bring in three or four cords of wood which they dumped in front of his saloon. When the crowd arrived from Tombstone for the speeches and the free drinks that went with them, Barton set off his bonfire. He marched up and down the Charleston street, ringing a loud cowbell. "C-c-come one, c-c-come all," he yelled. "I a-a-am a Re-Re-Republican, b-b-but I believe in f-f-free s-s-speech. M-Mark S-S-Smith and o-o-old scratch W-W-Wardell, the horses _____ of the Hua-Hua-Huachucas is g-g-going to m-m-make a speech in f-f-front of my p-p-place, and all you c-c-cowpunchers are w-w-welcome to f-f-free drinks, g-g-greasers in-in-included."

This incident was reported in the reminiscences of Mike Rice, an Arizona pioneer then working as a newspaperman in Tombstone. "Needless to say," commented Rice, "Jerry did the business of the evening to the chagrin of old Jake Swart. I was one of the Tombstone bunch who attended the function. The general was elected to the legislature that fall. . ." Mark Smith was also elected, became a famous attorney, and later was elected the territorial delegate to Congress, and was a United States senator. Mike Rice also mentions Barton in reporting the impromptu lynching of a rustler by a rancher who came upon the man in the act of re-branding one of his calves. The enraged rancher threw a noose around the rustler's neck, tossed it over a tree limb, and hoisted the unfortunate off the ground. Then he turned himself in. He was promptly turned loose again. Jerry's profane comment on the rustler's ancestry included the sentiment that "h-he h-had it c-c-coming."

When the Southern Pacific Railroad built its line across southern Arizona, it by-passed Tombstone by 25 miles to the north, where its railroad camp on the San Pedro River became the town of Benson. Then a spur line was laid along the river into Old Mexico, past the village of Fairbank ten miles from Tombstone, and Fairbank became Tombstone's rail connecting point. By 1885 Barton was running a saloon in Fairbank, and the Tombstone *Epitaph* on March 17, 1887, reported how his downfall began there.

Volunteer fire departments were usually the pet civic organizations of frontier towns, their only line of defense against that monster threat of destruction. The firemen practiced endlessly, their morale was high, and they were closely-knit personally and socially. So when the Tombstone fire department's chief engineer, Charles Tribolet, departed for a trip to Europe, his men gave him a going-away party when he boarded the train. According to the Tombstone *Epitaph* of March 17, 1887, the party was held in Jerry Barton's saloon in Fairbank. One of the firemen present was E. J. Swift, a man just over sixty years of age.

On March 16th Jerry Barton met Swift in front of the Fashion Saloon in Tombstone, and the two men argued over the settlement of a liquor bill stemming from the occasion of

Abandoned buildings in the ghost town of Fairbank, once the railhead for the town of Tombstone and the location of a saloon owned by Jerry Barton.

Tribolet's party. Angry words led to blows, Barton knocked Swift down, and Swift had Barton arrested. He was taken before the city recorder and fined eight dollars, which he paid. Shortly thereafter the two men met again in front of the St. Louis Beer Hall, the quarrel began again followed by another fight. Barton caught Swift by his beard, struck him two or three blows to the head and neck, and threw him out into the street. Onlookers picked up Swift and carried him across the street into the store of Mcneil, Moore and Co., where Swift was employed, and tried to resuscitate him. It was useless; in less than two minutes after Barton struck him, Swift was dead.

Chief of Police Oaks had seen part of the fracas; he arrested Barton and conducted him to the slammer. An autopsy showed that Swift's neck had been broken in two places. The coroner's jury report said that his death was caused by Barton's blow, and this time Barton was in for it. Swift was generally well-liked, left a widow with no means of support, and was much older than Barton. This time the sympathies of the community were with Swift. The fire company conducted an ornate funeral in which practically the whole town joined, and the grand jury indicted Barton for manslaughter. At his trial in November, he was convicted and sentenced to three years in Yuma penitentiary.

"I was at the penitentiary in Yuma when Barton was serving his time," states Mike Rice, who, of course, was not an inmate himself. "Bob Hatch was captain of the yard in charge of prison labor [the same Bob Hatch in the back of whose saloon Morgan Earp was assassinated years before in Tombstone], and he always seemed to me to be very harsh on Barton for some reason I could never ascertain. They were both booze-venders from Cochise County, Hatch in Tombstone and Barton in Charleston, and I imagine their interests conflicted. I was under the impression Barton worked against Hatch when he ran for sheriff, an office to which Hatch was elected. However, I know that he gave Jerry the hardest tasks in the cards, wheelbarrow and pick and shovel work. With the lovely Yuma sun beating down on poor Jerry's 250 pounds . . . it did not tend to enhance Jerry's affection for the captain of the yard, yet Jerry never kicked or shirked the tasks imposed upon him. He was always good-natured and popular with the inmates."

Present-day scene at the ghost town of Fairbank. Note the bare adobe wall in left background and adobe building at right.

Barton was pardoned by Governor Lewis Wolfley, and his citizenship thus restored, on March 21, 1890. He moved to Prescott with his wife, Sarah, and took up his old occupation again, running a saloon on the town's famed Whiskey Row. Here he was involved in another incident worthy of note. "A band of Salvation Army lasses came to Prescott," relates Mike Rice, "and attempted to save the souls of (the inhabitants of) that irreligious precinct known as Whiskey Row. With cornet, drum and tambourine they would collect a crowd of rough-necks in front of the . . . joints on the strip, enter the dumps, and shake their tambourines under the noses of the faro dealers and crap shooters.

"They became somewhat of a strain on the nerves of the saloon men, so they then tried to bar the lassies from the sidewalks in front of their places. The city marshal ordered them to move off the streets under pain of arrest. The lassies sought out Jerry Barton and put up to that lover of fair play their grievances. . . .

"Jerry informed them, 'L-l-ladies, this is m-m-my s-s-saloon and this is m-m-my s-s-sidewalk, and y-y-you girls c-c-can c-come and p-p-pray and s-s-sing all you p-p-please, and no d-d-damned s-s-skunk will b-b-bother you as l-l-long as I'm a-a-around." So with this assurance the Salvation Army lassies found a refuge from the tyranny of the other saloon keepers of Whiskey Row. Yet under Jerry's promised protection the girls did not always go unmolested.

"One night while the lassies were in the midst of their most solemn moment of exhortations, a big, six-foot cowpuncher with a ten-gallon hat, Colts on his hips, and spurs ripping up the sidewalk, elbowed his way through the crowd and, using the vilest brand of vocabulary, grossly insulted the Salvation Army girls. Barton was standing by, and walking up to the big stiff caught him by the collar and whirling him around like a boy's top, got this tirade off his chest.

"Y-y-you big _____, I a-a-asked those w-w-women t-t-to come into m-m-my p-p-place, and I p-p-promised them p-p-protection, and no b-b-bum of your g-g-grade can i-i-insult them. I v-v-vowed that I w-w-would n-n-never hit a man with m-m-my f-f-fists again, but b-b-by God I c-c-can use my f-f-feet." And suiting the action to the words, Jerry kicked the fellow in the belly and knocked him to the sidewalk, to the cheers of the assembled multitude. This ruffian was the notorious "Shoot-em-up Dick" that Jim Sam put out of commission in Globe, . . . and wound up later in the penitentiary. Jerry Barton did the best night's business, physically and financially, of any wet-goods joint in the 'Mile-High City' on that occasion."

Apparently Barton tried to mend his ways and settle down for good, as the Prescott newspapers printed occasional items about his family, including the birth of three children, one of whom died in infancy. We may assume that Barton mellowed, as there seem to be no further accounts of brawls with Barton involved after that time.

The incident involving "Shoot-em-up Dick" Mofford and Jim Sam in Globe, mentioned above by Mike Rice, was described in the reminiscences of Charles M. Clark, an Arizona pioneer who lived for some time in Globe. Jim Sam was a restaurant man, a Chinese who at one time or another ran an eating joint in every Arizona town worthy to be called one. Having been run out of Globe as an undesirable, "Shoot-em-up Dick" walked into Jim Sam's place in Pinal City and ordered the best meal in the house. He cleaned off the crockery to the last crumb, ordered one of the best cigars, and after lighting it sauntered toward the door without even looking at the check stand. Jim Sam reminded him, "Hey, you forget something?" "No, you blankety-blank so-and-so, I didn't forget nothin'—I'm Shoot-em-up Dick." Jim Sam seized a large horse–pistol. "So?" he inquired. "You Shoot-em-up Dick, I shoot-em-down Sam. You pay plenty quick." And Dick paid up.

You will, without doubt, agree that Charley Bennett qualifies as an Arizona character, though part of the reason his memoirs are included here is his interesting recollection of Jack Swilling, whose story is found elsewhere in this book. Bennett was born in Fort Smith, Arkansas on June 4, 1851, and arrived at Fort Verde, Arizona, in 1875 with a letter of recommendation to the quartermaster there. While waiting for a job to open up, Bennett worked at other occupations and left a rambling account.

"I met Happy Jack McAllister at about the time the Tiptop mine was struck," wrote Bennett. "He said, 'Let's go to Tiptop,' so we rigged up and went. We ran into old Jack Swilling there. We went to Gillett, the mill town, and looked around. I started a saloon and introduced the first liquor into the camp... I went to Prescott and got ten gallons of whiskey—it was wheat whiskey; had something to it. I had a tent on the opposite side of the (Agua Fria) river (from Gillett), so I put a keg on a rock and had a faucet in it and sold the whiskey for two-bits a swallow. Everybody wanted to know where that whiskey was, so I ordered some more. Then I put up a shack and got some more liquor. They drank up everything but some extracts, and I buried them. I had to take old Jack back to his camp.

"Jack was a great fellow, he took a liking to me. There was lots of shooting around there but he always stood by me. One day a fellow got sick and we got some whiskey for him. We also had a lot of butter, valuable as diamonds, in boxes. This cuss got to shootin' and some of the other fellows took to shootin' the butter, so I said to Jack, 'Squelch that fellow; shoot a man or two but don't shoot up the butter.' Old Jack got up, pushed him into a corner and said, 'You stand there and we'll shoot this out.' But he didn't. We weren't looking for any trouble.

"One day Jack Swilling called his little girl in, and he handed her a dagger and made her raise her right hand with the dagger in it. He said, 'Georgia, I'm going to swear you,' and he told her if anybody shot him in the back she was to kill him, but if he got shot in the face, it was all right. . . He sent for me and asked me to marry Georgia. I said I wasn't going to get married. She was awfully pretty, but she was very young, only about fourteen. . .

"I got my camp going about the time of the Tombstone excitement. . . A friend of mine came along and said, 'Let's go to Tombstone.' That was about 1878. I told him to go down to Phoenix and I would follow in a few days. But when I was living on the Verde River I had gotten to know an Arkansas girl, so when I left to go to Phoenix I was riding along, out about three miles, when that Arkansas girl got into my head, and I turned right around and went back to the Verde. Strange how little things change a man's life. . .

"Well, when I got up to the Verde I met the girl's father. He said he wanted to go back to Arkansas, and I said I would go with him. But I went to work for old George Hance, who had a ranch. . . I had a contract to furnish hoe-cut hay. George ran for justice of the peace, and he told me, 'If I am elected, you are

Large rock building, probably the store, still stands at the Gunsight Mine where Fred Wall was once the superintendent.

the first man I am going to marry.' I asked him, 'Who am I going to marry?' Well, George was elected, and he also made property assessments for tax purposes. One day he stopped by the ranch where I was working, to assess the ranch, and he said, 'How about that agreement that you would be the first man I would marry?' I was standing in front of the house, so I called out 'Annie!'—Annie Delts was her name—I said, 'Annie, come, let's get married!' You know, I had never talked to her before about getting married. It did look funny. But then George came in and said, 'He promised to get married; where are the old folks?'

"They came out, and said, 'You wouldn't get married that way, would you?' I was covered with mud all over, but I said, 'Yes, why not?' . . . But I went in and changed my clothes and said, 'Let's get this business over, I've got a lot of work to do. Come out here, Annie!' And so we were married; then I put my working clothes back on and finished my work." Before leaving George Hance, though, we should note that his brother John had come with him to Arizona in 1868. It was John Hance who took up a ranch on the rim of the Grand Canyon, built the first hotel on the canyon's rim and the famous Hance Trail from the rim down to the Colorado River.

"About that time," continued Bennett, "I made up my mind to go to Tombstone, so I bundled my outfit in the wagon and started. But coming out of Tempe I got on the wrong road and came into Sacaton. There I met some men who asked if I was going to Tombstone. I said I was, but they told me I'd never get there because of the Indians. This must have been in 1880. So I went to the Silver King Mine near Pinal City and worked two years in the mill. I intended to start a cattle business, but my wife got sick and died. We had had a little son, so I took the boy to some relatives in Texas, came back, and worked two years in the mine.

"The mine began to go bad, with cave-ins and fellows getting killed, so I told the boys, 'This is my last night.' They said, 'You can't quit,' but I replied, 'Oh, yes I can.' So I went to Jack Ryan. 'Jack,' I said, 'I want $500.' So he took a sack down from off the wall, with three or four thousand dollars in it. I told him I was going to buy out old Jim Foley, who had a big saloon. I paid Foley the $500 down and took it over. Then I emptied the bottles out into the creek. When the boys came in from the shift (in the mine) I said we had two kinds of drinks, beer and gin. Well, do you know, there were six weeks I never saw a bed, just slept on the billiard tables. I stayed right by the saloon and never closed it night or day. I made about $20,000. At last the camp went down (because of the falling price of silver). Then a firm wrote to me to come to Morenci; they wanted a man to take charge of a saloon there. I went, but didn't stay long. It was a tough proposition, lots of knocking (fighting) among the Mexicans, Portuguese, Italians. There were very few Americans."

Charley Bennett then found his way to Casa Grande, having probably worn out his taste for excitement. Bennett settled down on a farm near that city and became one of its most solid and dependable citizens. He was elected justice of the peace, and served on the school board and many offices of civic responsibility.

A contemporary of Bennett in Casa Grande, Charlie Eastman, left an account of the Arizona adventures of Fred Wall, who qualifies as an Arizona character because of what happened when that usually genial soul was aroused. He went from slow burn to berserk with no stage in between, and stayed that way until friends intervened. Wall was born in Detroit but arrived in Arizona in the early 1870s. Early in 1883, Eastman and Joe Cummings, on their way to the Gunsight Mine near Ajo camped at the Gunsight Well, six miles from the mine, to rest their four-mule team. Fred Wall was running a store there, and Eastman's first acquaintance with him was hearing Wall tell a drunken Yaqui Indian that he would put two bullets through his rotten carcass before he hit the floor. "I got pretty well acquainted with Wall," said Eastman, "as I married his wife's sister and associated with him more or less for 25 years till he died in Tucson."

Wall had been ranching in Nevada when he killed a man in a dispute and, said Eastman, "skinned out for Arizona, where identities were easily hidden and pasts soon forgotten (sound familiar?)." Fred went to work at the Quijotoa gold mine south of Casa Grande, where he worked with a bunch of Irish miners. He got into a fight with one of them, and was getting the best of it until the other Irishmen jumped in. Fred went down to his cabin and got his rifle. As he stepped outside he saw the whole

Ruins of rock building at the Gunsight Mine where Fred Wall was the superintendent and Charlie Eastman a worker.

Irish mob standing on the mine dump jeering at him. He fired a shot that went right through one Johnny Moran, laying him out, while the rest of the mob ran for shelter inside the mine. The Pima County sheriff arrested Wall, who was convicted of the charges and sent to Yuma penitentiary. He didn't stay there long; a petition for a pardon was circulated and many signatures obtained, including that of Moran, the man he had wounded.

Wall's next trouble came at the Silver Bell mine, northeast of Tucson, where he and Jim Fagan shot two Mexicans. Fred's good luck held again," said Eastman, "as the six-gun he had contained only two shells." Otherwise he would have killed many more of them, according to Eastman, who claimed that despite these deadly intemperate sprees Wall was generous and ruggedly honest. "He was always ready and willing to join a party searching for someone lost in the desert, and he knew every foot of it.

"An old prospector entered his store one time and bought grub, saying he was going to prospect along the Sonora line on this side (of the border with Mexico), as he had heard of placer diggings there. Fred gave him all the information he knew, including the name of an Indian village and little towns on the other side of the boundary where the man could find boundary markers. He also gave him a letter of introduction to the Mexican line-rider, in case he should happen to mistakenly stray across the line. . .

"Fred had just received some dry goods from Los Angeles, including a dozen silk handkerchiefs. The prospector bought two of them, and before departing said he would return in about two weeks for some tools if he found anything worth working on. When the prospector failed to return as expected, and Fred could find nothing of his whereabouts, Wall became worried. Then one day a young Papago Indian came into the store wearing one of the handkerchiefs the prospector had purchased. It aroused Fred's suspicions, and he asked the Indian where he obtained it. The answer was evasive, so Fred sent for the chief of the village where the Indian resided.

"The chief questioned the young buck closely and obtained a confession that he had killed the prospector to obtain the neckerchiefs he admired so much. Fred wanted to send to Gila Bend for an officer, but the chief refused, announcing he would

Mine shaft at the Gunsight Mine, named for a nearby mountain that seems to resemble a gunsight.

see the young Indian did not murder any more white men. So the chief, with some other Indians, some miners from Gunsight, Fred, his wife and her sister, followed the young Papago to the place he had murdered the prospector. Then the chief shot the murderer and both were buried in the same grave. Justice was swift in those days.

"While Fred was working at a gold mine 30 miles south of Casa Grande, the company fell behind in its monthly salary payments to the miners. Knowing Fred had the nerve to collect it, they asked him if he would attempt to get their salaries. Fred slipped into the boarding house and, without the knowledge of my wife or me, obtained my double-barreled shotgun. At the stamp mill he held up the boss and, while the rest of the mill men were scrambling out the back door, Fred got the men's pay by taking the bullion. When my wife saw him standing in front of the mill with the shotgun cocked, she went out and took it away from him before he could do any more damage.

"Fred was superintendent of the Gunsight gold mine, and my wife was running a boarding house for the workmen. Papago Indians stole and killed three hogs, which rooted out of and strayed from an old Indian wickiup in which we had penned them. We learned the identity of the thieving Indians and sent word to them to come in and pay for the hogs. They replied they would come in and clean us out, but would not pay for the hogs, as they had found them in the desert in dire need of water. So we made preparations for their 'cleaning-out program.'

"Fred, Sam Donaldson, Tom Day and others, all crack shots, were secreted behind an adobe wall with rifles. When the Indians approached, armed to the teeth, my wife put our three children under the bed out of the range of bullets, and we went outside. She had a six-gun under her apron, so we were two additions to the reception committee. When the Indians came close enough to see our arrangements, their fighting impulse suddenly left them. Two old chiefs discussed terms with my wife, finally agreeing to bring in three steers in exchange for the hogs. That was satisfactory to her. That's the kind of wives the Arizona pioneers had. . . real helpmates and comforts to their husbands and children. . . Women had nothing to fear from men in the early days of Arizona. They were respected and worshiped by the frontiersmen. . ."

Then there was Ben Reagan, one of four discoverers of the fabulous Silver King mine, located near the Pinal City of that day, and today's town of Superior. In 1884, after the discovery of the mine but before it became an active producer, Reagan was a hotel keeper in Florence. Attached to the hotel was a bar. There one night Reagan had an altercation with a discharged soldier who became very abusive and threatening. Reagan drew a knife and stabbed him to death. The next day he made the coffin for the victim, and being a Campbellite preacher officiated at the funeral, leading in the prayer and delivering the sermon.

Ruins of residence made of native stone at the Gunsight Mine.

Chapter 7

They Called Her "The Major"

First and foremost, no matter what else she was, Pauline Cushman was a woman. Wondrous and extraordinary, she was above and beyond everything else a woman. An Arizona pioneer newspaperman and sometimes law officer, Mike Rice, who knew her well for much of her life, described her as "a woman of magnificent physique, large, lustrous, sloe-black eyes, raven ringlets falling almost to her waist, with the profile of a Madonna, and a voice as melodious as a lute." At the time of that description, she was thirty-six years of age. She was at times warm and loving, haughty and disdainful, hated fiercely, loved deeply, and came to tragedy trying to hold on to the affections of the husband who was the love of her life. Of all the women who lived in Arizona Territory, Pauline Cushman's life story was the most sensational.

Pauline Cushman, actress, Union spy and wife of Jere Fryer, once sheriff of Pinal County, as she appeared in mid-life. (Courtesy Pinal County Historical Society)

She was born Hattie Pauline Cushman in New Orleans in 1835, and the first record of her life is her marriage in the "Magnolia House" in that city, in 1853, to Charles C. Dickinson.

They had two children, Charles L. who was born in 1858 and died in 1864, and Ida who was born in 1860 and also died in childhood. Her youthful beauty had helped launch her on a career as an actress, and she became famous, traveling all over the country and even to Australia, as a star attraction. Then the Civil War broke out, Pauline's husband joined the army, but died in Cleveland, Ohio, in 1862.

Pauline went back to the stage, and soon was starring in a war-time play, "The Seven Sisters," in Louisville, Kentucky. In one of the acts, the beautiful Pauline, in a military uniform, drank a toast to the Union cause. Residing in the town at the time were a number of young southern officers, on parole. They did not like the toast, but they certainly did like Pauline. One day some of them suggested to her that she change the toast and drink to "Jefferson Davis and the Southern Confederacy." She laughed at the idea, laughed at Davis and the South, and then they dared her and promised to pay her $500 if she delivered the toast that evening. This account first appeared in a San Francisco newspaper on December 3, 1893.

"The recompense was so great for what she regarded as a trivial piece of folly made the young actress suspicious and she hesitated," said the article. "It had not occurred to her that there was anything but a political joke in the escapade, as it was first proposed to her, but when the offer for money was made she put off the experiment for a night or two. Her frequent conferences with the Southern officers had been observed by the police, and one afternoon Pauline found herself summoned before General Boyle, the military commandant at Louisville. The general called on her to explain some suspicious circumstances. He alluded to the fact that she had a brother in the Confederate army. As a Union commander, he felt obliged to ascertain if her own sympathies ran with or against the Confederates.

"Pauline looked him up and down and laughed. Then she asserted her loyalty to the Union cause, and in doing so narrated the story of the boys who wanted her to direct the toast to Jefferson Davis. In telling this story to General Boyle, Pauline took the step toward making herself a Union spy in the war of the great rebellion. . . The chief of the army police at

Nashville wanted the services of a woman spy to penetrate the lines of the Confederates. General Montgomery believed that Pauline was the woman to take the risky commission. He offered it to her, she accepted, and then it was arranged that she should comply with the request of the Southern officers, shout for Jeff Davis in the theater, get arrested and drummed out of town, and go to Nashville and repeat the act of treason. The actress obeyed the instructions to the letter."

When she stepped out of her stage role to offer a toast to Jeff Davis, the audience went into an uproar. A Union captain helped her to escape the mob. The theater manager fired her for causing a riot, leaving her in the position to accept the assignment as a spy. Romantic stories of "the lovely young actress who was persecuted and driven out of two cities (Louisville and Nashville) by the Union soldiers filled the South," continued the article, "and she was the Confederate heroine of the hour."

Her cover was a pretense that she was hunting for her "lost brother," as she traveled from camp to camp. A southern captain became interested in her, and gave her a safe conduct letter to the South's General Bragg. Pauline stole some of the captain's papers and concealed them in her shoes. When she tried to get back to the Union lines, she could not find the pass to General Bragg, and was taken into custody and to General Morgan. She seized a chance to escape by jumping on a horse and heading for the Union lines, but was caught by a sentry and taken back to the Confederates.

She was brought before General Nathan Bedford Forrest, who ordered her to be taken to General Bragg at Shelbyville. The stolen papers were found in her shoes, but still Pauline would admit nothing. While she was being held for court-martial, she fell dangerously ill with a fever. As she lay ill, her guard informed her that she had been sentenced to be hanged as soon as she had recovered from her sickness. The Union forces, however, suddenly moved on Shelbyville, the Confederates had to quickly evacuate, and in the confusion Pauline escaped and returned to the Union forces with the information she had risked her life to gain.

"Her work being over," concluded the newspaper article, "the actress-spy broke down once more, and for weeks she lay

. . . near death. During her long sickness one of her most constant attendants was an army officer named Garfield, and it was he who subsequently wrote to President Lincoln an account of the black-eyed spy the boys had dubbed 'The Major.' 'Let her keep the title,' wrote Lincoln in reply. A year later, Lincoln was assassinated and Pauline Cushman was forgotten. Two decades after that the officer who had befriended her met a similar tragic fate, and the American nation went into mourning for James A. Garfield."

Lincoln's order that she be allowed to retain the title "Major" stayed with her for the rest of her life. A special examiner's report dated December 14, 1892, stated that "on account of Pauline Cushman's services, and bravery and pluck, she was called by President Lincoln the 'little Major' and that nom de guerre has stuck to her . . ." She was very proud of the title and insisted that everyone with whom she came in contact use it when referring to her.

After the war, Pauline resumed her acting career and was immensely popular. She organized her own troupe and went on an extensive tour of Western cities and mining camps. Everywhere she was met with acclaim and great success. In San Francisco she met up with Mike Rice, who had just returned from spending some time in frontier Arizona as a newspaperman in Phoenix, Tucson and Tombstone, and as correspondent with soldiers fighting the Apache wars. ". . . In the fall of 1871," says Rice's account, "I secured a place as bellboy at the Grand Hotel in San Francisco, then the most famous hostelry on the Pacific coast. I answered the beck and call of the great and near-great of that period, who patronized that elaborate rendezvous of bonanza kings, railroad magnates, senators, actresses, politicians, and the breed of hangers-on who attach themselves to reckless spend-thrifts. . . .

"It was in this environment that I first met Pauline Cushman. . . In company with Dr. Samuel J. Orr, then her affianced husband, she came to California to fill a theatrical engagement at the old Metropolitan Theater . . . I will here digress to state that Dr. Orr was then on his way West to report for duty as army surgeon at Camp Bowie, Arizona. It was Dr. Orr who performed that historical surgical operation on the arms of Johnnie Dobbs, shot to pieces by the Apaches. . . His boneless arms could manipulate a six-shooter or a billiard cue with the dexterity of a movie wielder of a gun of today. Dr. Orr's and Pauline's romance came to naught, as they never saw each other again. The doctor contracted a fatal illness, and I think died at Camp Bowie. He was a sterling gentleman. . .

"To get back to the events leading to my association with the Major, it was my fate, or fortune, to be the bellhop who answered the first call of the newly-arrived guests, Dr. Orr and Pauline Cushman. While they occupied separate sleeping apartments, they had in common a reception parlor, where they received visitors, and admirers theatrical and otherwise. To this parlor I was directed by the chief clerk who received the tube call (no phone in those days, they just blew their messages down a pipe line).

"On entering the reception room, I found a number of people seated around a large center table, one of whom I recognized as John McCullough, the most famous tragedian of that or any other time in thespian history. Another was Tom Fitch, the famous silver-tongued orator of the West, well-known to all old-time Tucsonans. (Tom Fitch was a famous attorney who practiced in several Arizona towns, among them Tombstone, where he defended Wyatt Earp at his court hearing following the gunfight at the O. K. Corral).

"Pauline asked me if she could have allotted to her a special servant, to wait on her during her sojourn at the hotel. I informed her that such could be arranged by calling the chief clerk. She scrutinized me closely and after a few questions as to my knowledge of the city, especially the theaters, she went to the tube, called the chief clerk and asked to have me allotted as her special attendant, and I entered the Major's service forthwith. Thus was my acquaintance with Pauline Cushman formed and a friendship welded that held firm through prosperity and adversity until her death.

". . . My duties were to accompany her to and from the theater . . . and look after her wardrobe, which was entirely military, as her characters in 'The French Spy' and two other plays that she produced were entirely masculine. Her make-up as an army officer was perfection itself and her rendition of the characters superb. Her engagement lasted a month and the proceeds were satisfactory. After her engagement ended, Dr. Orr left for Camp Bowie, and Pauline left her apartment at the hotel and moved to less expensive quarters where she devoted her time to writing her memoirs, but these efforts never reached a publisher as far as I know.

"Feeling that my services were valueless to Miss Cushman, I parted with her—though grudgingly on her part—and went on the road with Lotta Crabtree who succeeded the Major at the Metropole . . . On my return to San Francisco I sought out Pauline, but learned she had left the city, gave up the stage, and never returned to the theatrical profession." It may have been that during these months Pauline had married again. The official records state that she married August Fitchner in San Francisco on December 19, 1872, a marriage that ended with Fitchner's death.

"I finally located her at a place called 'La Honda,' a fashionable resort some miles south of San Francisco," continued Mike Rice. "A man named Sears, owner of the hotel, engaged the Major as 'manageress' of the resort, and there I found her 'monarch of all she surveyed.' As a hostess she was popular and a social success, although her regime terminated in a very abrupt manner. Sears became infatuated with his 'manageress,' and persistently forced his attentions on her. The man was absolutely repellent to her and she firmly resisted his advances. His actions became so unbearable that she tendered her resignation as hostess of the hotel. This so aroused Sears' ire that he went about the community saying many untruthful and scandalous things about his relations with her. Of course his lying remarks reached her, so she bided her time for her revenge.

"She notified the guests of the resort that she would leave the place on a certain morning and requested them to be on hand, on the departure of the stagecoach for the city. I assisted her in packing her things and carrying them to the stage as soon as it arrived at the hotel entrance. There were many guests present and a number had already boarded the stage, crowding it to its capacity.

"The stage driver was in his seat, lines and whip in hand, shouting 'All aboard!' I got on top of the stage behind the driver, and was in a good position to see what I knew was about to take place. The Major was still on the hotel platform, the driver urging her to get aboard. Bill Sears was bowing and scraping to his departing guests and passing wisecracks to the throng. Suddenly Pauline came up to the side of the stage and, calling the driver by name, asked him to see his whip. The driver handed her the whip and quicker than it takes to tell it she began lashing Sears over the head and shoulders with the six-horse whip. She laid it on good and heavy, and would stand no interference until she completed a genuine horsewhipping on her slanderer. Sears carried the marks of the lashing on his face for many days.

"The California press carried great scare-headline accounts of the horsewhipping of Bill Sears, and I recall the *San Francisco Chronicle* carried the account of the Major's combativeness with the heading of the article 'A Traducer Trounced.' This was the first fighting stunt of the Major of which I was cognizant, but not the last. . .

"Pauline returned to San Francisco where she led a sedentary life for several months. Later she moved to Santa Cruz, California, where she entered into partnership with a man named Bill Chandler. They located two timber claims in the Santa Cruz Mountains. These claims contained some of the largest and finest redwood trees in that great timber belt. They built a large log house, furnished it comfortably, and for a time entertained extensively during the fishing and hunting season. However, the partnership was dissolved, the Major receiving a very liberal settlement for her interest.

"She moved to Santa Cruz where she got into another conflict with a would-be admirer. I was not present, but I got the details from an eye-witness. She did not use a horsewhip on this occasion, but she piled on the unfortunate's head all the delft (crockery) on a dining room table. The man was a popular character in Santa Cruz, and it was generally conceded that Pauline's action was uncalled-for and a great indignity heaped on a reputable citizen. Her action in this case lost her many friends. She soon after left Santa Cruz, and I did not see her for four years. I next met her and was her guest at San Gabriel Mission where she kept a roadhouse or tavern and seemed to prosper financially."

At San Gabriel, Pauline met Jere Fryer, a prominent young man of the community, handsome and stalwart, partly of Cherokee Indian lineage, and fifteen years younger than she. Pauline became deeply infatuated with him, and he was attracted to her, at a time when her beauty was not what it once had been, as she was nearing forty-five years of age. For some reason, which does not seem to be recorded anywhere, the pair left San Gabriel for frontier Arizona. Perhaps, as Mike Rice suggests, it had something to do with the railroad building across Arizona Territory. The official record shows that Pauline and Jere (also known as Jerre and Jeremiah) were married in Florence on January 29, 1879. This was four months before the Southern Pacific railroad suspended construction for a time, because of the summer heat, in May, 1879, at its newly-named way station of Casa Grande in the middle of the Arizona desert.

Jeremiah (Jere) Fryer, Pauline Cushman's husband, sheriff of Pinal County (1887-1889). (Courtesy Pinal County Historical Society)

Pauline and Jere were already there, two of five people in the little town with only a few adobe and board-and-batten buildings. "They settled at the station," continues Mike Rice's account, "Fryer engaging in the saloon and livery businesses," and Pauline running the famous Fryer Hotel. "It was at Casa Grande that Mrs. Fryer pulled off some of her more aggressive stunts. . . Her reputation as a scrapper had preceded her to Arizona. Women in particular feared and shunned her as much as possible, and some men had good reason to fight shy of her when she was on the warpath." Because of her jealousies, Jere's affections were waning, and willful Pauline was ready to, and did, use every womanly wile and fighting tactic to keep him.

"One case I will cite to which I was a witness," continues Mike Rice. "Pauline had a tender spot in her heart for man or beast who was being mistreated. Casa Grande was the shipping point for Florence and the Silver King mine. The big freighters were usually quartered at Fryer's corral. Mrs. Fryer was always watchful that animals were not overloaded or mistreated on leaving the corral. One day a teamster known as 'Blue' hitched up a team of sore-shouldered mules and was about to put them in the lead of a string of twenty animals. Mrs. Fryer accosted 'Blue,' and protested against him working animals in that condition. He told her 'they were his mules, and it was none of her damned business anyhow.' She replied, 'I'll make it my business, and you won't take this team in its present condition out of this corral.' He said, 'I will take them out, and what are you going to do about it?' She parleyed no longer with 'Blue,' but went into the house and returned with a Winchester rifle and, throwing it down on the mule-whacker, forced him at the muzzle of the gun to unhitch the sore-shouldered mules and substitute another team. This act on her part was generally approved by teamsters who were more humane than 'Blue,' and it tended to take starch out of a bully.

"She had many verbal encounters with men and women in Casa Grande in which she came out best, as she was generally on the right side of the issue. However, . . . her Waterloo came at Casa Grande, and that from an irate lady possessed of fighting ability superior to the 'Major.' Pauline was jealous of Mr. Fryer's rumored association with other women, and with some reason. She accused a neighbor woman of undue intimacy with Fryer, which Fryer strenuously denied. This lady, hearing of the Major's aspersions, sought her out in the mule corral, and there occurred as lively a donnybrook as ever was witnessed by an admiring assemblage of roughnecks. Jere Fryer with a few cronies, including myself, watched the combat through cracks in the fence, and he was visibly affected at the finish. . . The Major took the count with disheveled tresses and darkened optics. Her defeat robbed her of her reputation as a combatant in Casa Grande." Reports of other incidents in Pauline's life while she lived in the town are to be found in the chapter on Casa Grande, elsewhere in this book.

Pauline Cushman House in Florence, still occupied, was the home of Jere and Pauline Fryer during his term as Pinal County Sheriff.

Jere Fryer was elected sheriff of Pinal County in November, 1886, and he and Pauline moved to Florence, the county seat. Mike Rice, who had been Pauline's attendant and whose account of her life we have been following, also moved to Florence as county jailer under Fryer. His reminiscences recall a night in August, 1887, when Fryer and all his deputies happened to be out of town at the same time, and Rice was the sole custodian of the sheriff's office and the jail. He and the county attorney, Richard Sloan, were sleeping on cots outside the sheriff's office because of the extreme summer heat, when at about eleven

Original Pinal County Court House in Florence, now McFarland State Historic Park. Porticos added in 1904 now obscure the old sheriff's office, which was at the extreme left.

o'clock Rice was awakened by a hand gently touching his forehead. It was Jeff Bramlet, one of those harmless ne'er-do-wells who made a poor living by doing chores around the saloons. Mike Rice, irritated at being wakened, asked what the blankety-blank he meant by waking him at that hour.

Bramlet whispered that he came with a "tip" that the vigilantes were holding a meeting, that they knew the sheriff and his deputies were out of town, and were coming to take four suspected murderers from the jail and lynch them. Mike asked Sloan what he should do, but Sloan refused to get involved, and Mike was left on his own to meet the threat. He decided to investigate first and, slipping on his trousers and shoes, crept around to the meeting place. It was in the "tunnel," an underground excavation with a canopy roof in a livery corral behind the Tunnel Saloon, used for card playing and drinking. Rice crawled cautiously up on the canopy, from where he could see nothing but could hear everything perfectly.

Several people spoke for and against the lynching, but it was finally decided to storm the jail, overpower Rice and get his keys, take the prisoners from the cells, and hang them. Rice had heard enough. He retreated down the alley to the jail, and was able to find only two people to help him hold off the vigilantes. One was a Dave Gibson, whom he stationed in a vacant room across the street from the jail with a sawed-off shotgun. The other was Pauline Fryer, whom he woke, and who promised to hurry to the jail as soon as she dressed. Arriving there, she took her station in her husband's chair in his office, armed with a six-shooter and a rifle. Still there were only three against a mob, but Mike Rice had an idea.

He woke the prisoners and described the situation to them. Then he proposed that he arm the prisoners themselves in their own defense, if they would promise that, when the danger had passed, they would give up their arms peacefully and return to their cells. All gave him their promises, and Rice gave each of them a Winchester rifle with a full magazine plus a handful of extra cartridges. He took a sawed-off shotgun for himself, and all went upstairs to the grand jury room over the sheriff's office.

The sashes had been removed from the two windows for summer ventilation. Rice stationed the prisoners so they could shoot down through the window openings if it became necessary. He called down to Pauline that they were ready, and she called back, "So are we. You do your part and Dave and I will do ours." Just then a mob of forty to fifty men rounded the corner and headed for the sheriff's office. Rice stepped to the window, shotgun in full view, and called on them to halt. Taken by surprise, they did. "I have beaten you to it," proclaimed Rice. "I have four deputies with me to protect the jail and its contents, so you advance even a yard at your own peril." Seeing the armed men with Rice, the mob scattered. The prisoners, after some none-too-gentle persuasion by one of them, returned to their cells.

"... At Florence," continues Mike Rice's account of Pauline's life, "the Major was in constant turmoil over Jere's supposed infidelity. She was inordinately infatuated with her husband and resorted to extraordinary methods to retain his affections, waning (because of her) exceeding jealousy. She was many years older than he and age was making inroads on her once beautiful features, adding to her discontent. It was at Florence a matter transpired of which few people were cognizant. It was kept from Fryer's knowledge out of sympathy for him, as he was a kindly, generous, and popular man.

"Pauline finally conspired with a woman from Picket Post (near today's town of Superior) who was about to become the mother of an unwanted child to get the baby and pass it off on Fryer as his own. The heartless woman left for San Francisco, where the Major was to join her later and consummate the conspiracy. Pauline led Fryer to believe that she was about to become a mother (remember, she was now about fifty-two years old) and induced him to permit her to go to a maternity hospital in San Francisco. She was gone from Florence for several months.

"One day Fryer entered the sheriff's office with one of his aides, bearing a letter from Mrs. Fryer telling him of the birth of a daughter and announcing a soon return to Florence. Never was a man so elated as he was at this glad tidings, and he celebrated the event regardless of expense. Mrs. Fryer with the baby soon ... arrived home, and was exultantly received. Fryer announced himself the happiest man in Arizona, and nothing was too good for the mother and baby. Its presence brought a complete reconciliation of the couple. He showed an almost fanatical affection for the baby, as did Mrs. Fryer.

"The little girl was baptized and christened 'Emma,' and for once Jere became a home-loving devotee... The poor little child was afflicted almost from birth with an incurable nervous disease and suffered terribly. I have seen Fryer take the little spasm-attacked baby in his arms and walk the floor for hours at a stretch, while Mrs. Fryer wearied out and would try to get a little repose. I have often carried the sick child in my arms, and on one occasion a spasm attacked her, her little limbs contracted, and she actually bounced out of the cradle onto the floor. Death eventually put an end to the little one's suffering, the fraud became public, and it ended in the complete separation of Mr. and Mrs. Fryer."

Mike Rice has his timing wrong in his report, as the fraud was exposed and the separation of the Fryers came before the death of the little baby. The reminiscences of Alice F. Curnow in the Arizona Historical Society tell of her arrival by railroad in Casa Grande in the late 1880s. These reminiscences are to be found in the chapter on Casa Grande elsewhere in this book. She stayed at the Fryer Hotel, which Pauline was again running at that time, and describes the tiny baby and its condition then. Therefore, the deception had been exposed and the Fryers had separated before the baby's death, and Pauline had returned to Casa Grande with the child. She soon moved back to San Francisco, and whether the baby's death occurred in Casa Grande or San Francisco is unclear. Pauline never returned to Arizona.

"The last time I met Pauline was in San Francisco," continues Mike Rice, not mentioning the year which must have been 1890 or 1891. "In company of B. J. Whitesides I called on her at the Baldwin Hotel. She was quartered in a magnificent suite of rooms at that high-priced hostelry. After our visit she commanded me—and I mean that word—to call again in the afternoon as she had an important mission. Even then, a command from the Major brooked no denial. I returned late in the afternoon and she handed me a sealed letter and told me to take it to the box office of the Baldwin Theater and there await a reply.

"As it was but a few steps from her apartment to the theater lobby, I went forth and presented the missive . . . The letter contained a request for a pass for two for the coming performance. (It) was addressed to James Ward, the famous actor, who was then playing an engagement at the theater. He happened to be in the box office at the time . . . and expressed astonishment to find his boyhood friend and preceptor was alive and in the same building with him. He ordered the ticket clerk to issue a proscenium box pass to Pauline and any party she chose to accompany her to the show.

"I brought her the pass, and she then ordered me to get ready to escort her to the play that night. This I declined to do, but she insisted, . . . so I consented to appease her whim. At this period in Pauline's life many features of her youthful attractiveness had passed. Her face had become wrinkled, her tresses gray, and she resorted to artifice to hide the blemishes. She prepared at once to doll up for the occasion by calling a beauty artist, had her face enameled and her hair done up in colonial style. She dressed in a flowing robe of black satin, topped off with a broad-brimmed Gainsborough hat with two white ostrich plumes.

"With her statuesque figure she looked every inch a queen. I preceded her to the theater lobby and we were ushered into a proscenium box on a level with the stage, the most conspicuous place in that big and fashionable theater, overlooking the dress circle. She made me occupy a front seat with her. I was overcome with such a feeling of embarrassment that I wished there was some means to crawl... into oblivion. Every lorgnette and opera glass was trained on that box, as it was newsed around that Pauline Cushman, the spy of the rebellion, was an occupant. Any old Arizona burro puncher could appreciate how I felt. I was so badly shattered I don't know to this day the name of the play.

"Between acts she was visited in the box by prominent people, newspaper scribes, actors and actresses, and after the show she was taken in tow by James Ward and others for an after-theater supper at Taits... A few days later Pauline was hostess to Senator W. M. Stewart of Nevada, Sam Davis, editor of the Carson City (Nevada) *Appeal*, and others including James Ward, who as a youthful (actor) she sponsored in juvenile parts that finally landed him at the head of his profession. Senator Stewart had previously introduced a relief bill on pensions for $10,000 for the Major's services in the Civil War, and at the meeting described I heard him tell her she would get the relief asked for in the bill at the adjourned term of Congress. Pauline died before the relief bill could be considered by the House of Representatives."

Death came to Pauline Cushman on December 2, 1893, at fifty-eight years of age. Despite the above display of opulence, her obituary said she had been living for the three previous years at a lodging house at 1118 Market Street. Almost penniless, she had applied for a pension based on the military service of her first husband, Charles Dickinson. "She succeeded in securing, after long endeavors, a small pension for her valuable services during the war, and upon this she managed to exist," said the obituary. "For some time she had been suffering from sciatica in her knees and pains in the region of her heart. Yesterday morning about ten o'clock she was discovered by her landlady lying unconscious on her bed. Two physicians were immediately summoned. All their efforts were in vain, however, and she steadily sank until two o'clock in the afternoon when death came."

There was some surmise that her death was a suicide by poisoning, but it never was substantiated. Nor was any such test necessary. Fighters, survivors, battlers with Pauline Cushman's love for life don't go out that way. Hers was not a model life, but a full and rich one, and even the most valiant heart must eventually give way.

Chapter 8

Casa Grande is Twenty Miles from Casa Grande

General Antonio Lopez de Santa Anna, dictator of Mexico, was a troubled man in 1853. True, he had recently been restored to power after being tossed out of office and cuffed around by his own people after the Texas fiasco. In the meantime, there had been that unpleasantness with the United States, a war, at the end of which Mexico had lost all of California and its other territories north of the Gila River in New Mexico (of which Arizona was then a part) to the Yankees. The controversy over the international boundary still had not been settled, both sides sending troops to the disputed areas, with any minor incident likely to spark another war. But Mexico was broke, in political and economic turmoil, and Santa Anna had been resurrected to see if he could end the chaos.

Then in March an emissary from U. S. President Franklin Pierce arrived. His name was James Gadsden. His boss, Gadsden told Santa Anna, was anxious to end this impasse peaceably. Would the general accept ten million Yankee dollars for another small slice of Mexico's northern desert between the Colorado and Rio Grande rivers? The Texas cattlemen were clamoring for a border settlement that would provide a flat route over which to build a railroad to the stockyards of the burgeoning California cities. After all, the desert strip was hot, barren, and inhabited mostly by rattlesnakes, scorpions, lizards and a few peons. Santa Anna replied that he certainly would listen. Gadsden tried to get a seaport at the mouth of the Colorado, but Santa Anna drew the line there. No seaport, but the boundary was redrawn to its present location, the Yankees got their slice of desert, and Santa Anna his ten million dollars.

It was late in 1878, more than twenty-five years later, that

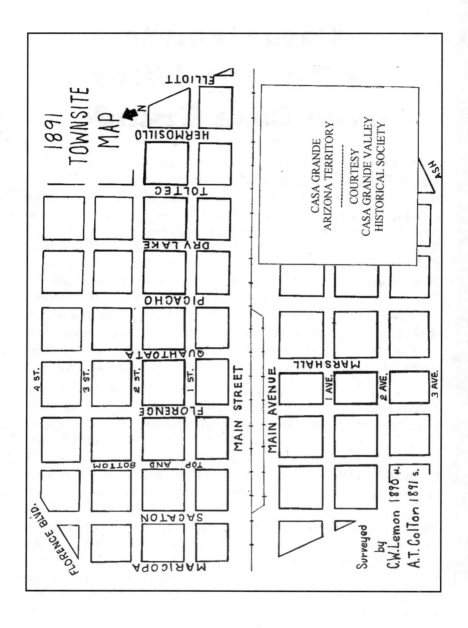

1891 TOWNSITE MAP

CASA GRANDE
ARIZONA TERRITORY

COURTESY
CASA GRANDE VALLEY
HISTORICAL SOCIETY

Surveyed
by
C.W.Lemon 1890 N.
A.T.Colton 1891 S.

the Southern Pacific railroad began laying its line eastward from the Colorado River across the Arizona desert toward El Paso, Texas. Some matters had to be attended to during those twenty-five years, including a Civil War and the subjugation of the Apache Indians, through whose territory the railroad must run. The rails ran near the Gila River for a time, but gradually drew away from it until at Maricopa they were eight miles south of the old Butterfield Overland Trail that ran along the Gila, and the old stage station at Maricopa Wells. Then the rail route turned gradually to an almost directly northwest-to-southeast alignment to rejoin the overland trail near the present town of Eloy and follow it, sometimes directly in it, to Tucson.

As the rail roadbed was building eastward from the Colorado, permanent way stations and sidings were left at Gila Bend and Maricopa. A small string of cars followed the railroad crews over the newly-built portion, and wherever it stopped it was a rail station called "Terminus" at which railroad business was conducted, and passengers and freight were taken on or let off. As the telegraph line was also building alongside the tracks and the trains carried the mail, "Terminus" was sort of a rolling, temporary station gradually moving eastward just behind the construction sites.

By the middle of May, 1879, the desert heat was building, beginning to take its toll on the construction crews. Mostly they were Chinese laborers, whose basic food was rice, evidenced by great piles of rice sacks left at intervals along the line. On Saturday, May 17th, the contractors delivered as completed the 27 miles of roadbed they had built from Maricopa. The railroad accepted it, and decided to suspend construction for the summer. At the present end of the track, a new way station would be established. What to name it? The officials looked around. There was no prominent landmark anywhere in sight after which to name it, only miles of sand, greasewood, and low desert hills. Twenty miles northeast was a curious sight that many travelers went out of their way to behold. On the desert were great buildings of caliche earth, one rising to four stories high, built by a long-vanished race of primitive Indians. They were called the "Casas Grande" (big houses), and so the new way station was given the name Casa Grande.

Ancient Indian Ruins at Casa Grande National Monument for which the town was named. Protective steel canopy was erected by the federal government.

According to an anonymous monograph in the files of the Casa Grande Valley Historical Society, it was the next day after the Southern Pacific took over the new portion of the line, on Sunday, May 18, 1879, that the railroad, Western Union, and Wells-Fargo Express Company offices and personnel moved with "Terminus" to its newly-named station, Casa Grande. The following day, Monday, May 19, the first official train pulled in, bringing in the first freight, mail and express, and inaugurating the first telegraph service.

Surprisingly, all this was met by the germ of a town. There were a few buildings and five residents. This came about because the whole of Arizona Territory was watching the railroad's progress with avid interest, and there had been some accurate guesses that a new station and town would be established at the Casa Grande site. Two of the earliest settlers were the famous Jere Fryer and his wife, Pauline, who, as Pauline Cushman, had been the celebrated actress and a spy for the Union during the Civil War. There seems to be no record of how this famed couple happened to settle in the tiny railroad town in the middle of the desert. They had been married in Florence, the town nearest Casa Grande, and perhaps were looking for a place that seemed to have a future to make a home (see chapter on Pauline Cushman).

Coming in with the railroad were Arthur H. Elliot, Western Union telegrapher, and A. J. Wright, Wells-Fargo agent. Frank Souba ran the Gilt Edge Saloon, Jack McCoy and Robert "Bat" Bolen operated livery stables, Smith and Watzlavzick ran a general merchandise store as did Buckalew and Ochoa, whose store manager was unequal to the task. He was soon replaced by Perry Wildman, who arrived in Casa Grande on July 4, 1879. His reminiscences are to be found in the Arizona Historical Society. "As I stepped from the mixed train of freight and passenger cars," he wrote, ". . . I surveyed my surroundings and saw three buildings. One was the store of Buckalew and Ochoa, another the store of Smith and Watzlavzick, both wooden buildings and good-sized. The other was an adobe, about 12 by 20 feet, the famous hotel of Jere Fryer, and was recommended to me as the best-kept hotel in the world, and also the largest because there were plenty of cots and the corral was sufficiently large. . .

"As I stood on the platform of the railroad station I saw two men emerge from the adobe building, each holding an American flag in one hand and a Colt six-gun in the other. It was about eight a.m., but the sun had already been up four hours, and it must have been about 'tenth drink time.' At any rate, these men marched along the street waving their flags and shooting their guns, to the B & O store which they entered, and soon came out of with a man between them. It was a German fellow in charge of the B & O store whose place I was to take, and a sort of recluse, of quiet and retired disposition, not inclined to drink. Well, they marched along in noisy fashion to the adobe building, and the (man) was forced to drink to the great American bird and several other patriotic institutions. These proceedings (occupied) most of the forenoon and I, being somewhat frightened, remained in the shade of the station, talking to the agent, who assured me that there was no danger, that the two men who were celebrating were the leading citizens of the town, Jere Fryer and Louis DuPuy. As the population was only five

Original railroad depot at Casa Grande. It first stood in Yuma, but was dismantled, shipped to Casa Grande and re-assembled about 1885. It was destroyed by fire in 1937. (Courtesy Casa Grande Valley Historical Soc.)

persons, it was incumbent upon them to see that our national anniversary was properly remembered. . .

". . . After the demonstration had subsided, . . . I ventured across the street to the hotel and met the hostess, Mrs. Fryer. She immediately put aside any fear I had and kindly assigned me a cot and the privilege of sleeping in the house or the corral (because of the summer heat). I chose the house first and later adjourned to the corral. I was delightfully surprised in meeting Mrs. Fryer. I had seen her many years before in New York as Pauline Cushman on the stage. . . and now as a tenderfoot in this out of the world place I adored her for the courteous and motherly way in which she made me comfortable. I afterward became acquainted with Louis DuPuy who had charge of Smith and Watzlavzick's business. . ."

The first post office was established July 31, 1879, with Charles Dane as postmaster, succeeded on September 10th of the next year by Jere Fryer himself. More pioneers were arriving at Casa Grande, among them John C. Loss, agent of the

Arizona Stage Company, Jimmy Woods who opened a saloon and whose wife operated a restaurant and later the Woods Hotel, and the Stiles family, whose son Billy became famous both as a lawman and outlaw. "With the railroad the town boomed and grew overnight," the anonymous monograph continues. "Gunfighters, outlaws, horse thieves, skinners and freighters rubbed elbows with the homesteaders, ranchers, and pioneers," a description that would apply to almost any frontier town in the West. Casa Grande was the shipping point for supplies to the famous mines for miles around, the Vekol silver mine and the Quijotoa gold mines to the south, and the fabulous Silver King mine to the northeast near today's town of Superior.

In October, 1879, the railroad began building again toward Tucson, and reached that point on March 17, 1880. There were no stations or sidings along the way, which was gradually upgrade from Casa Grande's 1,400 feet elevation to Tucson's 2,390. This led to a startling event late in 1881, recounted in the reminiscences of the Casa Grande station agent and telegrapher at the time, Arthur H. Elliott. "Late in (one) evening," he recalled, "a heavily-loaded freight train pulled into Tucson, but left five cars on the track while the engine and the rest of the cars went on to the yards. As you know, it is downgrade all the way (to Casa Grande) from Tucson. Something accidentally started those five cars, and they were on their way to Casa Grande gathering momentum and velocity with every revolution of the wheels.

"About the same time No. 19 passenger train from the west with high officials of the railroad aboard her was expected. Along about midnight, I was about to leave the office, when the telephone jangled. The excited voice of the Tucson operator came over the wire, "Is No. 19 coming?" "Yes," I replied. "Then hold her at all costs or there'll be the devil to pay!" (cried the Tucson operator). I ran out and threw the switch just as the headlights of the passenger train shone in the distance. Then I flagged the train. In the meantime, a light engine had been sent out in pursuit of the runaway cars, but returned with the report that nothing was to be seen.

"The brakeman and fireman of No. 19 were very impatient to be on their way, scarcely believing my story of the oncoming cars, but I told them my orders were to hold them. Engineer Ingram, of Oakland, and the conductor, Mr. Patton, climbed up on the engine and went to sleep. On the siding, to where I had thrown the switch, stood a carload of wood. At about two a.m. I heard a mighty roar. "Here they come, boys!" I yelled. The foremost of the cars was loaded with steel rails, which projected over the front of the car. As they dashed at a speed of about sixty miles an hour through the open switch they struck with terrific force the car of wood, a million sparks illuminated the sky while the rails were twisted like paper and the wood car demolished.

"Had those projecting rails struck the engine of the passenger train, the boiler would have been penetrated and exploded, and the whole train would have caught fire with a serious loss of life. Sleeping in the train were the big officials of the railroad; Mr. A. N. Town, general manager, was one. He rose from a brakeman to his position as manager. The passengers never knew of their narrow escape from death until the next morning in Tucson."

As an aside to this incident, you may have noticed that Elliott, the station agent, stated that as he was about to leave during the night "the telephone jangled." At first glance one would think Elliott had a lapse of memory, and that it was the telegraph key that began chattering. References are, however, that the telephone was invented in 1876, and that in 1881 the first commercial switchboard was installed in Tucson. There were some private phones in Phoenix as early as 1882, but the first commercial switchboard there was installed in 1891. So it is possible that there was a telephone line running through Casa Grande as early as late 1881.

Though the Casa Grande town site wasn't created for another ten years, when the patent was signed by President Benjamin Harrison on August 8, 1892, the southwest quarter of it was growing in sort of cockeyed fashion in the early 1880s (see illustration). Rather than the regular north-south, east-west layout, the main streets and most businesses were parallel to the railroad tracks running northwest to southeast, with the depot on an island in the railroad yards. North of the tracks was and is Main Street; on the south side Main Avenue. Beyond them were the usual First, Second, Third, etc., Streets, and

First, Second, Third, etc., Avenues.

At right angles to the frontages, the principal streets were Sacaton, Top and Bottom, Florence, Quahtoata, Picacho, and Dry Lake. Top and Bottom Street came by its name from the gamblers that patronized the saloons and gambling halls who swore that they could not tell whether the cards dealt to them came from the top or bottom of the deck. Now it has a more civilized name, Washington Street. Quahtoata was the butchered spelling of 'Quijotoa,' a Papago Indian name for a mountain to the south where there was a mine. South of the tracks, for some reason, it was Marshall Street.

One of Arizona's and Casa Grande's most noted pioneers, Charles J. Eastman, arrived in town in 1884 according to his reminiscences. "When I arrived in Casa Grande in 1884," he wrote, "Pauline Cushman was here, running a hotel at the corner of Main and Top and Bottom Streets. 'Major' Fryer, as she was known, was a square shooter, good-hearted and an excellent nurse in taking care of anyone injured by bullet wounds. Also, she was a woman who always wanted to see fair play.

"I remember the killing of Price Johnson about 1885. I saw the 'Major' standing there with her 'forty-five' (caliber pistol), to see that each of the combatants, Johnson and a man named Robinson, had fair play. Robinson killed Johnson. During the shooting 'Major' Fryer stood there on the corner, the bullets whistling past within fifteen or twenty feet of where she was standing. At no time did she flinch.

"I recall still another interesting episode in connection with 'Major' Fryer. One night as I was going along the street drunk, I encountered the old 'Major' at the corner of Top and Bottom Street. The 'Major' stopped me and asked if I had seen that 'long-legged husband' of hers, Jere Fryer. I replied that I did not keep track of other women's husbands. No sooner had I spoken than she pulled her 'forty-five,' cocked it, stuck it up against my belly and said, 'I asked you a civil question and I want an answer due to a lady.' It seems to me I got sober in a hurry and answered, 'No, "Major," I have not seen Mr. Fryer.' 'That's the way to answer a lady,' she remarked, and to my great relief took the 'forty-five' away from my grub sack. That was the kind of timber (she) was made of, afraid of nothing, open and above board in every way, always ready to help her fellow men out. No one ever went hungry or wanted a bed while the 'Major' was alive." Unfortunately, in later years, Pauline failed to live up to Eastman's assessment of her.

Eastman's reminiscences continued, "In the spring of 1884, the town ... was wide open with plenty of money in sight. It was the shipping point for the Quijotoa, Vekol, Silver Reef, and others (mines) to the south. A few men who were killed in Casa Grande, among whom were Price Johnson, Pricherd and Uncle Ben Drew, I knew personally. I have had several funny personal experiences, but I will just mention two which will illustrate early conditions.

"My partner, Isaac Williams, a trader at Sacaton (a Pima Indian village), had ordered some grub from Tom Tomlinson who kept a store (in Casa Grande). We were to take a four days' trip south to locate an old mine. It was Christmas time, our grub was in a sack for carrying convenience, and we had two gallons of whiskey. (Notice that for a four-day trip they took two gallons of whiskey, for two men.) We spent the night drinking and gambling, and we wanted to make an early start. Tomlinson told us to get the key from over the door and get our grub

This building replaced the first Tom Tomlinson store which was destroyed in the 1893 fire in Casa Grande. (Courtesy Casa Grande Valley Historical Soc.)

Gilt Edge Saloon, one of Casa Grande's original buildings, owned by Frank Souba. (Courtesy Casa Grande Valley Historical Soc.)

whenever we got ready to pull out. So early in the morning we went into the store, grabbed the whiskey and sack, and left. When we camped that night south of the Jackrabbit Mine we found that our sack of grub was a sack of onions—I had made a mistake in the sacks. So our Christmas meal that evening was whiskey and onions." While Eastman's tale is comical, the fate of Tom Tomlinson, the storekeeper, was tragic. He was run over by a train and killed while crossing the tracks. One version says he was sleepwalking, another that he was hard of hearing. A less charitable conjecture might be that he had spent too much time in the Gilt Edge Saloon or some similar establishment.

"Another incident along a different line happened while I was at Vekol," went on Eastman. "Deputy U. S. Marshal Will Smith . . . went to a (Papago) Indian village south of Vekol to arrest an Indian for murder. The Indians would not give up the murderer, so Smith came back to Vekol and got Lou Gillison and myself to help arrest the Indian. The Indians had been on a drunk and were ugly. They had us surrounded but finally promised me, and I knew them all, to bring the prisoner to Casa Grande on a certain day, which they did. I took up a ranch in this (Casa Grande) valley and with the flood waters from

Cockleburr Wash I raised everything. I lost my cattle in the drought of 1910 and quit ranching. . ."

Eastman went on to other pursuits during a long and useful life in Casa Grande. As a member of the Arizona Pioneers Association, he wrote of humorous reminiscences of early days in that town for the association's annual reunion, that are to be found in his file at the Arizona Historical Society in Tucson. Some of them are titled "Society News of Casa Grande in 1884":

January—*Joe Phy bending his six-gun over Montgomery's head, bi-secting it, for talking about Joe, and all the shock brought out was blood and corn meal mush. (Phy, a candidate from Florence for county sheriff, quarreled in a Casa Grande saloon with Tom Montgomery, a gambler from Globe, and pistol-whipped him.)*

February—*Billy Stiles, the bandit, and his brother Grant, fighting in their mother's house, while Charles Eastman was appropriating the old lady's ducks for his dinner.*

March—*Charlie Fay and Jack McCoy celebrating the seventeenth of Ireland by fighting, Charlie butting Jack in the stomach with his head until it disarranged the department of Jack McCoy's interior.*

April—*"Major" Fryer dousing Mrs. Cummings in the water trough for slander. Tin-horn gambler hitting George Melvin over the head with a billiard cue in Dick Bilderbacus' saloon, making George see stars in the daytime.*

May—*Grand ball in restaurant. Charlie Eastman and B. B. DeNure orchestra, guitar and accordion. Everybody got drunk. Unknown party sat down on accordion and smashed the guts out of it.*

June—*Old Man Bean, the wagon maker, traded four lots to Saxe, the stage driver, for his wife. Had an elegant wedding, married by Marshall, the judge. Everybody got soused and wanted to kiss the bride.*

July—*Everybody drunk on the Fourth. Dick Chillson*

tried to hold up the passenger train, when John C. Loss, the Wells-Fargo agent, drew down on him with a double-barreled shotgun. George Morse, the constable, knocked the eye out of a Mexican for resisting arrest. Bill Stiles and Ed Jane fought a duel back of the blacksmith shop, while Johnny Grass and John Cron staged another duel on Front (Main) Street. No casualties, visibility too uncertain.

August—*Charlie Eastman celebrating his birthday by getting stewed as a boiled owl. Tried to get under a big freight wagon at Bean's wagon shop. Got stuck in the loop of the lock chain hanging on to the side of the wagon, head and shoulders under the wagon box while the rest of him pointed to the sky.*

September—*Mexican holiday on the sixteenth. Lots of mescal, chili con carne and dancing with the senoritas. Everybody pickled.*

October—*Half of Casa Grande burned down. No way of getting sufficient water to fight the conflagration, except turning the wells upside down. Done the next best thing. Rolled a barrel of whiskey out in the street from Harry Holburn's grocery store. Knocked the head in and then with empty oyster cans helped ourselves singing "Hot Time in the Old Town Tonight."*

November—*Al Richerson's wife standing in front of her husband's saloon with a double-barreled shotgun. She had filled Al's carcass full of bird shot. Some misunderstanding in domestic affairs.*

December—*All the desert rats getting ready, priming their Arizona nightingales (burros) for a get-away out to the hills, to do their annual assessment work (yearly improvements to a mining claim to keep it from reverting to the government). The annual Christmas celebration not as bright and gay, owing to the absence of a number of prominent society leaders, they being out in the hills working on their claims, doing assessment work and preparing beans and sowbelly for their Christmas dinner.*

The foregoing doesn't resemble the formal society notes to be found in a regular newspaper, but they are all Casa Grande had then and reflect the town's lifestyle. It doesn't matter, either, that not all those happenings were in 1884. The October fire that destroyed half the town seems to be the only reference anywhere to that event, though you can bet there were efforts to fight it other than Charlie's tale of just watching while getting smashed. And Joe Phy did bend his six-gun over Tom Montgomery's head, but not in January, 1884. That occurred in September, 1886.

Phy was running for sheriff of Pinal County against M. W. Harter and Casa Grande's own Jere Fryer. Fryer won, and he and Pauline moved to the county seat at Florence, depriving Casa Grande of its two most famous citizens and their reflected renown. By the end of Fryer's term, he and Pauline had separated, and she returned to Casa Grande for a short time before going back to California. The Tucson *Arizona Daily Star* on November 16, 1889, said, "Mrs. Pauline Fryer has resumed charge of the Fryer Hotel. She is very attentive to guests and her house is very popular. Everything is kept clean and bright, and not only travelers, but residents of Casa Grande, appreciate her efforts to please." It was during this period that a young woman traveling by train to join her husband, a cowboy on a ranch in the Pinal Mountains, passed through Casa Grande. The memoirs of Alice F. Curnow provide fascinating glimpses of the train ride through a sandstorm, of the famous Fryer Hotel, and of Pauline Cushman herself.

As her train proceeded slowly eastward over the Arizona desert, the wind-whipped sand piled in drifts across the tracks, so that shovelers had to be sent ahead of the engine to dig down to the tracks. "Going in the opposite direction from that in which the storm was traveling, the train passed out of it," she wrote. "The sand had been rolled and curled beneath the violent blasts of the wind until its dunes were shaped like great snowdrifts after the wind has swept their sides into tiny ridges. In places these dunes were higher than the train. It was a monotonous journey, riding slowly between hills of sand, stopping in sheltered places for the shovelers to do their work.

"It was past midnight when the train stopped at Casa

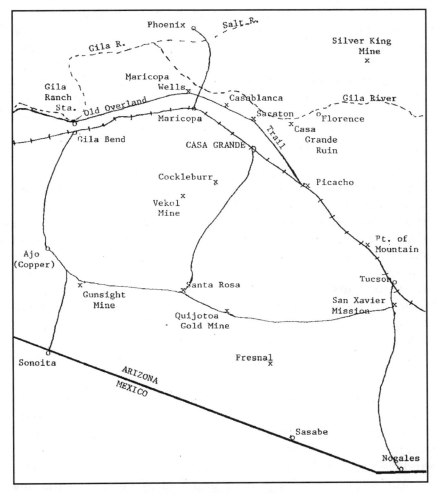

CASA GRANDE REGION, 1880s

Grande. The porter helped me off with my baggage and the train sped on its way. The few other passengers who had alighted seemed to have melted into the night, leaving me alone on the platform. The agent was locking the door of the baggage room when I asked, 'Will you please direct me to the hotel?' He pointed down the track, across the road to an adobe building that loomed above the outlines of the other little houses, saying, 'Right over there, miss.' Following his directions, I stumbled along the track until I reached the hotel, which consisted of a number of little, detached houses, each about eight feet square.

"A knock brought the proprietor to the door and with a lantern he conducted me across the extensive, brush-covered yard to one of them. As he stepped inside he turned to me, saying, 'Look out that you step high; that sill is five inches up.' 'Why do you keep it so high?' I asked. 'To keep out the water of the Gila River when it overflows its banks and that's pretty near every time it rains.' He placed my baggage on the dirt floor, lighted a candle on a chair without a back at the head of the bed, and withdrew from the room.

"As I closed and locked the door, I noticed a curtain hanging from a shelf behind it, of the same shade as the adobe walls that were in their natural color. There was no ceiling under the dirt roof. The small window opening with its small, round sticks set when the adobe was soft and were then immovable, reminded me of the bars of a prison. There must have been a similar opening at the rear of the building that faced the back of mine, for I could distinctly hear the conversation. One would say: 'Here! If you're going to play, ante!' 'It's your deal, Ned. Hell, if you are going to play seven up, pal, don't hold up the game.' 'Come on!' shouted another. 'Have a drink on Sam! He lost.' 'The hell I did! Frank lost it hisself, so he's inviting you all up to the bar. Come on!'

"As I listened, I sat down on the edge of the bed, from where I could easily have touched the opposite wall, and unhappily contemplated my surroundings. . . I heard my neighbor shout, 'Lights out!' after which all was quiet. . . Sleep was impossible, and I waited for daylight. At the first sound of activity outside, I cautiously opened the door and looked down the narrow passageway between the two rows of little houses like my own. All seemed to be occupied; all doors had been left open, no one except myself seemed to fear intruders.

"In the largest of the buildings I found Mrs. Fryer, the landlady. She was a hard-looking woman of forty-or forty-five (Pauline was actually at this time about fifty-five) years. She was washing a tiny baby before a smoking fireplace. The poor little thing was blue with the cold, as Mrs. Fryer explained that it was an adopted child and was about eight months old. From its appearance, I had judged its age to be about three weeks. As Mrs. Fryer flipped it over on its back upon her knee, it made no protest. It seemed too weak, as it drew its little skinny legs and arms up as tightly as it could. Its little chin was trembling, and its eyes stared straight ahead of it, paying no attention to anything.

"With the naked baby lying on her knee, Mrs. Fryer turned to me and said, 'My husband is Jere Fryer. He was sheriff of this county. I am Major Pauline Cushman. I was a spy for the Union army and for my work I received my commission from President Lincoln.' I wanted to cry out to her to cover the baby, but she was a woman one knew would take no suggestions from anyone, and it might be worse for the baby to interfere. With the child hanging over one arm, Mrs. Fryer walked to a table across the room and, picking up a book, she said, "This is the story of my life. You may have it for a dollar and a half.' At that moment, a man came to the door, saying, 'The stage is ready.' And I was glad to escape from Mrs. Fryer..."

Busy as it was as a railroad town, Casa Grande didn't have that depot, at which Alice Curnow arrived, for a few years after its founding. Five or six years after the tracks arrived at Casa Grande, according to agent Arthur H. Elliott, a new station was built at Yuma. The old one was dismantled, board by board, freighted to Casa Grande, and re-assembled there. It was a two-story wooden building, with second-floor living quarters for the station-master and his family. The station, an old-timer of the type so familiar in pictures, burned down in 1937. The present one replaced it in 1939.

Sometime after Pauline Cushman had moved away, back to California, Jere Fryer returned to Casa Grande from Tucson, where he had been living. He is mentioned in the reminiscences of a man who arrived in the late 1880s and remained for the rest of his life. Charles F. Bennett, one of the town's most useful and community-minded citizens, had come to Arizona in 1875. He was something of a rapscallion then, whose adventures are recounted in a previous chapter of this book. Bennett was running a saloon in the rip-roaring Morenci copper camp when a friend's letter urged him to come to Casa Grande.

"So I came to sell these boys a mine deal he (the friend) had on," wrote Bennett in his reminiscences, "but he wrote a letter that queered the whole thing. But I stayed on here and went broke, and have been broke ever since. I went in with Jere Fryer in the saloon business and he drank up all the profits. . . I had worked at everything, but the saloon business was the thing in those days. Even in the legislature nearly every last fellow of them was a saloon-keeper.

"I was elected justice of the peace in 1892; when I quit the saloon business things were so rotten they wanted me to become justice of the peace, and I had been in office only a week when I had eighteen men in jail. I said, 'You must remember that other people have rights as well as yourself.' I fined one man $100, and he said, 'I thought you were a friend of mine.' And I said, 'You don't think I'm going to let that interfere with the law, do you? If you say much more, I'll make the fine $200.' I located a homestead in the 1890s on which I since resided, continuously praying God that we could get water—still praying." Though he had only an eighth-grade education, Bennett was postmaster for ten years, a Pinal County supervisor, U. S. Commissioner, and school trustee on and off for years. Too bad we don't have memoirs from the Mexican pioneers of Casa Grande, whose lives were as colorful and useful as many from whom we do. Men with names like Jose Armenta, Ramon Cruz, and Robert Andrade among others were respected Casa Grande businessmen.

A filed clipping from an unidentified newspaper, dated October 9, 1893, reads: "Casa Grande was nearly wiped off the map of Arizona day before yesterday. Between seven and eight o'clock a fire broke out in a vacant building owned by D. J. Curry and in less than an hour the entire business part of the town was in ruins. The only means of combating the fire was by a hastily-organized bucket brigade and the only sources of water were the railroad tank and wells.

"The following is a list of the property destroyed: D. J. Curry, hotel and several buildings; Jack McCoy, livery corral and stables; Mrs. Tomlinson, two business blocks; E. P. Drew, building and stock of groceries, dry goods, and liquor; W. H. Green, building and saloon; a restaurant; W. C. Smith, general merchandise and two buildings filled with hay and grain; Jack Kramer, saloon building and fixtures, the stock was saved. The only property insured was that of Smith. Kramer's policy had

The Famous Fryer Hotel of Jere and Pauline Fryer first occupied the location where this hotel was erected circa 1890-93. (Courtesy Casa Grande Valley Historical Society)

expired the day before the fire and he refused to re-write. The total loss is estimated at from $25,000 to $30,000."

Casa Grande staggered back to its feet after that fire, only to be kayoed again by a big fire in 1914. Lest one think things were dull between the fire-caused frenzies, though, one needs only to turn to Charlie Eastman's "Social News of the Early Nineties" to be assured they were not. His notes are to be found in his file at the Arizona Historical Society:

> *"Mark Smith, our delegate to Congress, paid his every-two-year visit to the Republican microbes of Casa Grande, aiming to reform and domesticate them. During his visit the elite of the town staged a grand ball. Music was furnished by the orchestra, which added another instrument for the occasion. The jews-harp was a welcome addition to the accordion and guitar.*

> *"News that President Cleveland appointed our friend, L. C. Hughes of the Tucson "Star" to be governor of the Territory, reached here with rejoicing on every side. When the good word reached the town, everyone got*

saturated. The Pima and Papago Indians also took part in the celebration by getting filled up with red-eye.

"Tom Weedin, editor of the Florence Enterprise, paid us one of his occasional visits to show us our error in not voting the Democratic ticket. We all got "how come you so," and old Tom, being a Missouri Democrat, went away disgusted. He returned to Florence and gave us all a ripping up the back in his paper.

"Old Man Slavan, a Mormon survivor of the Mountain Meadows Massacre, was appointed official dog catcher for the town, including tomcats and roosters. Slavan seems to have a mania for sterilizing all males of the species and carries a sharp knife to perform his operations, and gets a great deal of pleasure out of his work.

"Some prospector brought a Gila monster (a poisonous lizard), about twenty inches long, off the desert, and made a present of it to one of our respected citizens, Jim Woods, proprietor of the saloon by that name. Jim's liquor dispensary was located south of the tracks, where the Casa Grande Hotel is now situated. In order to advertise his business, he had a sign painted on the window, "For Sale or Rent, one Gila monster, the most vicious and poisonous reptile in Arizona, and a half dozen imported red bats." The result of this was that Jim started doing a land office business selling booze to train passengers, exhibiting his Gila monster and a half dozen brick bats. Finally, someone put a chunk of ice in the box where the creature was confined and the poor reptile froze to death. This, however, did not interfere with Jim's advertising campaign. He rose to the occasion by putting the reptile in a jar of alcohol. This liquid took the hide right off it. Woods then claimed the thing was a deep sea monster caught off the coast of Lower California. Of course, all the boys that were around Jim's dive when he was exhibiting his curiosity to the suckers would wiggle in and irrigate (get drunk) at the tenderfoot's expense.

"There was no social function a roaring success

*without the ladies of Casa Grande taking a hand in it,
usually with "Major" (Pauline) Fryer acting as the
master of ceremonies. She made you toe the mark, and
if you failed you were liable to get a crack over the head
with her six-gun, a bottle, or anything else that was
handy.*

*"Another social leader was old Mother Stiles. She
was not as high-spirited as the old "Major," but when the
boys got too hilarious and pulled their guns, she would
gently slip up to the aggressor with her Arkansas tooth-
pick that had a nine-inch blade, or her flat-iron, and tell
him to take it easy or she would tap the claret.*

*"When the capitol was moved from Prescott to Phoe-
nix on wheels in 1889, our distinguished representative
from Pinal County, Louis De Pough (DuPuy?) got off the
train and set up drinks to all the boys. Johnny Bryson
accused him of being a Kentucky horse thief and Louis
neither confirmed nor denied the accusation. Both being
Kentuckians, we concluded that Bryson knew what he
was talking about.*

*"Jim Sam, a Chinaman but an American citizen,
gave a blowout in his hash joint. Jim was the presiding
high cockalorum. He kept his meat cleaver handy in case
any of the guests acted rough—Jim promptly proceeded
to turn him into chop suey.*

*"Charles Bennett, our genial postmaster and justice
of the peace, who has done more to civilize Casa Grande
and put it on the map, informed his friends that when he
left Arkansas in the seventies and came to Arizona in a
covered wagon, that he was very near six feet tall. The
sun and this arid climate has shrunk him to about a foot,
so in order to hold your original dimensions here it is
necessary to be hung, then your neck will stretch about
a foot.*

*"Two of the most estimable ladies in town seem to
have no neighborliness towards one another, and are
always quarreling across the picket fence and throwing
flat irons and washtubs in each other's direction. Their*

husbands finally built a board fence about seven feet high between their yards thinking this would stop the feud. This fence did not do much good, as they kept their argument and grievances going behind their forty-five Colts, taking potshots at one another through the board fence on any favorable occasion.

"Another familiar jasper around town was a long-haired old man named Dunbar. He was with Walker's filibustering expedition in Nicaragua (meaning a private raid on a foreign country). A very suave old gentleman and a favorite of "Major" Fryer, he came from the South, like she did. He, like the old "Major," believed that all difficulties should be settled behind old man Colt, and the man quickest on the draw was in his estimation a success, when the other fellow checked out. Whenever there was a society fracas down at old Mother Stiles' house, and the old girl was about to use her nine-inch frog sticker on somebody, old Dunbar would always back her up with his shooting irons.

"'Idaho Bill' was another conspicuous citizen. (When sober, he was W. H. Sutherland, owner of the Arizona Stage Line.) He could get on the outside of more coffin varnish than any man I ever knew on account of his legs being about five feet long and hollow. The booze would settle down in that part with the result that his extremities would get drunk first. When Idaho couldn't circulate anymore, he would lay down in a convenient place and warble "Home, Sweet Home." When Mrs. Idaho heard that her hubby was in a suspended state of animation, she and a big two-hundred-fifty-pound Papago squaw named Martiana would make their appearance upon the scene of her spouse's playground with a wheelbarrow. She and Martiana would roll Idaho in the vehicle and then, tandem-like, with she in front pulling on Bill's legs and the squaw behind holding the handles and pushing the conveyance, they would get him home, dump the old boy in a stack of grass hay, and leave him alone in his slumber.

"One more old turtle, named Brewster, was a shining light (he was bald-headed) in Casa Grande social activities. Brewster's presence at any social gathering was very conspicuous, as his dome did not have any more hair on it than an egg. This assisted in brightening up the gloom, as it were. As long as he stayed in town on his jamborees he was all right, even if he was thrown in the box-car jail frequently. But when he went to Florence and got drunk, Pete Gabriel, the sheriff, would put him in the chain gang in spite of his strenuous objections to such undignified proceedings. In order to evade working on the streets, our hairless friend would cut the seat out of his breeches. The sheriff, not to be outwitted in this contest, bought a new pair of overalls every time this happened and made Brewster get busy in the chain gang. However, the county got tired of buying breeches for the old man and told him to get the hell out of Florence, get back to Casa Grande, and decorate their jail.

"Of all the men I knew in Casa Grande in the early 'eighties and 'nineties, I knew of but one who died a natural death. That was an Irishman named Donovan. The other boys died of lead poisoning (getting shot), or else dried up and blew away. Old Donovan had no lungs when he came here. All he had was a mean disposition on account of being raised on potatoes and goat milk. He was as convincing a liar as ever spilled a windy yarn. Knowing his time was short, he asked us boys to hold a regular Irish wake over the remains when he cashed in his last chip. The wake that was held in his shanty was one that will linger long in the memory of the ones attending. The old fellow was laid out on planks on top of a dry goods box, and a half dozen of us sad and mournful looking jaspers sat around with a jug of red-eye whiskey handy, waiting for him to cool off. Bill Fitzgerald, better known as Windy Bill, was sitting at the feet of the corpse.

"All of a sudden he up and made a jump right through the window, telling us at the same time that he saw Donovan's leg jerk. That movement started the stampede for the door and in no time there was not one *mourner left in the room for they were all making a rush for the thirst parlor with Windy Bill bringing up the rear, so fast and sudden were the movements of the rest of us. We found the horse doctor in the saloon playing poker, and promptly told him of the phenomena. After a few swigs of joy water all around to allay the excitement and soothe the wrought-up nerves, the doctor accompanied us back to the shack, and found old Donovan still there with candles burning and the jug of lollydrops where we left it in our mad rush out the door. We stayed and finished the wake and the jug after the doc explained that sometimes in a dead person a movement of the muscles is caused by the relaxing of certain nerves, and in this case no doubt the leg was moved by this cause. He also told us that we did not have to worry as the old fellow was too dead to skin.*

"The pioneer ladies of Arizona mixed with the rough and ready men in a way that would, no doubt, shock the more prude and frighten the timid woman of today. In every true man there is an instinct to protect, honor and respect womanhood. Here on the outer edge of civilization, the men appreciated and felt the refining influence of the noble women who braved the dangers of the new country, suffered the heat of the desert, and put up with the hardships of this frontier in order to make a home for their men folks. It was the tender touch of their hands that dressed the wounds, their gentle voices that commanded men to carry on, their loving arms that reared the youth, and their love, care and devotion that transformed a dry wilderness into a home surrounded by a rose garden. For these reasons their will was obeyed and even the worst of the bad men yielded to their suggestions. They had nothing to fear from these men, as they were respected and worshiped in the Territory of Arizona."

Applause is in order for Charlie's social notes, and a special round for his last paragraph. The old, devil-may-care days of which he wrote are gone forever. The town of which he wrote is not, however. Today, because of the ills of the railroads, it has turned its back on the tracks that nurtured it and its attention toward Interstate Highways 8 and 10, a short distance from the town to the south and east. A drive down Florence Boulevard, Casa Grande's new main street connecting it with the freeways and lined with chain motels and fast food joints, won't do much to lure the tourist. But the charms of Casa Grande, it's clean and orderly business district, modern subdivisions of homes, and relaxed and casual desert atmosphere, certainly will. And for the discerning, there is the chance to relive the town's Western history by visits to its "old town" section.

Casa Grande sort of shot itself in the foot in that regard with a "renovation" of the old town during which some of the historic buildings were torn down. There are some of them left, however, enough to intrigue those—and there are a lot of them—interested in traces of the Old West. At a stop at the Casa Grande Valley Historical Society on Florence Boulevard, the visitor can view exhibits showing "how it was" in the town's early days, and pick up some literature. Among this is a free brochure that is a walking/driving tour of the old town, describing the history of buildings still there, and showing the locations of famous ones that are gone.

Among them are the homes of Tom Tomlinson, John Loss, and M. E. Souva, the old Casa Grande and Sacaton Hotels, the sites of the old adobe school and of the first Catholic and Protestant churches. Also marked are the locations of the famous old Fryer Hotel, the Gilt Edge Saloon, and the original railroad depot. Marshall Street is marked as first being "Quahtoata" Street, but nothing identifies Washington Street as once having been "Top and Bottom." That's a shame; Casa Grande could do more, but the Historical Society is trying. We are all indebted to them for preserving and identifying its Old West heritage as well and as much as it has.

Sometime you should do it. Walk down Main Street and Main Avenue. Cross the famed Southern Pacific tracks at Florence Street and spend some time seeing the old town. It won't take much imagination to have Pauline Cushman and Jere Fryer, Tom Tomlinson and "Idaho Bill" Sutherland, Charlie Eastman, Arthur Elliott and Judge Bennett walking beside you, telling you how it was there when Casa Grande was young.

Chapter 9

Life & Death
in the
Desert

Rarely, praise be, does anyone die of thirst in the desert anymore. Though the southwestern two-thirds of Arizona is part of the vast Sonoran Desert, and thousands of people live in and around it, familiarity has not bred contempt but understanding and respect. The invention of air conditioning had very much to do with it; people are not inclined to move around on the desert as much as they might when it was hot everywhere. If travel in the desert heat becomes necessary, modern, high-speed freeways and automobiles with advanced water-cooling circulation and air-conditioning systems have removed most of its perils.

It has been that way only for about the last fifty years, we all know. Before then, anyone traveling in the desert had to know how far it was to the next waterholes or wells, and carry enough water with him to sustain himself and his animals. Miscalculation usually meant death from dehydration, exposure and thirst. There was no radio call for help, no highway patrol, no sheriff's posse of searchers, no circling aircraft. The traveler and his beasts of burden simply lay down and died.

What was it like to die of thirst in the desert? About fifty years ago, a man set out deliberately on a desert journey, tramping a well-marked trail, believing that he was well-prepared and secure though it was a hot day. Some slight deviations from his plans left him without water, resulting in a narrow brush with death from thirst. He survived to describe his experience. First, he said, you are powerfully thirsty, thirstier than you have ever been in your life. You can't keep your mind off it. You stop sweating, and your skin begins to dry out. Having heard of putting a couple of pebbles in your mouth

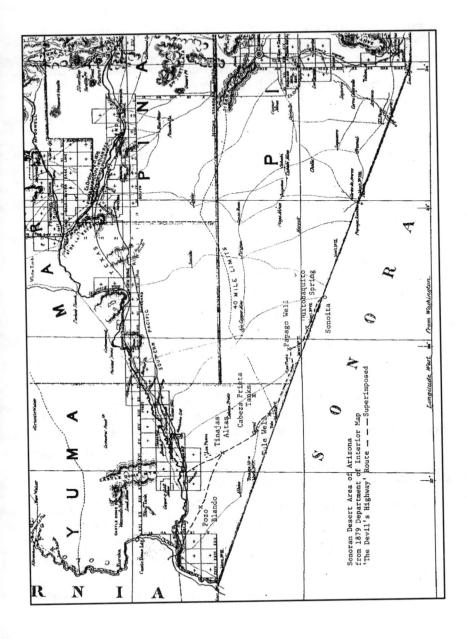

Sonoran Desert Area of Arizona
from 1879 Department of Interior Map
'The Devil's Highway' Route — — Superimposed

to stimulate the flow of saliva, you try that. They rattle around in your mouth like a pair of dice; there is no saliva to flow. Your lips dry out and crack open. Your tongue swells up until it is too big to stay in your mouth.

You feel the need to throw up, but there is nothing there, and your esophagus is dry all the way down. You get hot all over and want to shed all your clothes; those who have done that have all died. Your mind begins to wander; the mind of this traveler centered on anything wet. He fancied that he heard water faucets, brooks, rain, snow on the window. He felt that he was in a hot oven. Managing to find shade in an arroyo, he sat down, and heard a gurgling in his pack. It was a can of tomatoes he had forgotten he had. That was enough to allow him, after the sun had gone down, to stagger on to his destination, saving his life.

About one hundred years ago Capt. D. D. Galliard of the Army Corps of Engineers, a member of the commission marking the boundary between the United States and Mexico, wrote of the commission's experiences and the effects of the sun on desert workers and travelers. Hard as it may be to believe, the boundary workers were working during the hottest part of the year in the desert, the temperatures were 130 degrees in the sun at eight a.m., and reached 160 degrees at one-thirty p.m. "In spite of the large quantities of water drunk," he wrote, "the fact remained that one's thirst was never entirely quenched, due . . . more especially to the fact that the very dry air when (breathed) absorbed moisture from the throat and glands during its passage into the lungs, creating in those parts . . . a sensation of plain, every-day thirst."

It seems incredible that men could live and work in such heat, but they did. "In such temperatures the average quantity of water . . . consumed in twenty-four hours was about six quarts per man," he wrote, "but in times of arduous work and excessive temperatures over nine quarts per day were consumed by some of the men. . . The animals, when engaged in very hard work, averaged twenty gallons each. In the middle States, under similar conditions of work, a man would consume about two quarts and an animal about eight gallons during this period." From the above, the problem of just transporting along enough

Grave marker on El Camino Del Diablo, "The Devil's Highway," north of Tinajas Altas, 1958. (Copyright Wayne Winters, Arizona Historical Society.)

water for man and beast to survive while merely traveling, not even working, in such desert heat becomes apparent.

What about the stories saying that desert travelers desperate for water can chop off the top of a cactus, and find inside enough water to sustain their lives? Two words will suffice—forget it. The stately saguaro is not the fabled plant, but the smaller barrel cactus, usually attaining a height of three or four feet. There is no water inside the cactus, but it has been said that chewing the gummy pulp will yield enough moisture to alleviate thirst. Capt. Galliard destroyed the myth outright. "This is not the case, for any desert traveler who has once tasted the vile sap of this cactus and prefers it to death must, indeed, dread the terrors of such a death," he wrote. "... As it is difficult to cut into its interior unless provided with an axe or hatchet, two things a lost traveler seldom has, and as its sap must be strained through a cloth to separate it from the pulp, as this sap is neither pleasant nor wholesome, and as this cactus is entirely absent from the portions of desert most distant from water, its efficacy as a life preserver has been much overestimated."

The obvious answer to death from heat and thirst on the desert is not to go there during the extremities of temperature in the summer. Life couldn't stand still for six months of the year, however, in early Arizona any more than it can now. People's lives had to be lived, no matter what the dangers. So they prepared as well as they could and braved those dangers. The specter of death was a constant companion on Arizona's desert roads. Perhaps the worst of all the roads crossing the most blazing deserts and claiming most of the victims, was the notorious "El Camino del Diablo," or "The Devil's Highway," in extreme southwestern Arizona.

This road began at Sonoita, Mexico, on the boundary, and ended at Yuma, Arizona, at the confluence of the Gila and Colorado Rivers. It was first explored by Spanish conquistadors and traveling priests, seeking an overland route from Mexico to their colonies on the California coast. For long stretches of its one hundred and twenty-five miles the road ran on the American side of the border, within sight of the border itself, before veering northward toward water holes, and reach-

*Cabeza Prieta tanks in the Cabeza Prieta Mountains near El Camina Del Diablo, "The Devil's Highway." Man is unidentified. (*Copyright Wayne Winters, Arizona Historical Society.)

ing the Gila River. It skirted the harsh, low desert mountain ranges, the Agua Dulce, the Sierra Pinta and the Cabeza Prieta, to swing northwesterly on the east side of the Tinajas Altas range.

Water was found naturally along the way at Quitobaquito spring, Papago Wells and Tule Well. In the mountains, large "tanks" worn into the solid rock by centuries of exposure to the elements filled with enough water during the infrequent rains to serve travelers' needs until evaporation emptied them again. Some were so large, and fed each other through a series of tanks from the upper crags to the lower, that they seldom were emptied during the driest seasons. This was particularly true of the Cabeza Prieta tanks, a series of six natural tanks, the higher draining into the lower, so large that it was possible to water a thousand animals in a short time. It was estimated that they held 5,000 gallons of water. Similar tanks were found in the Tinajas Altas (High Tanks) Mountains, where again there was a series with the higher draining into the lower through a series of natural waterways.

Capt. Galliard described the Tinajas Altas tanks in his account. "A more reliable supply (could be found) at Las Tinajas Altas, fifty-six miles from Yuma, where the waters of occasional rains were collected in a high mountain canyon, and, passing through a narrow rocky gorge, hundreds of feet above the ground, came tumbling down the rocks in a series of cascades. At the foot of each of these, during the course of countless ages, a deep, circular basin had been worn in the solid rock.

"Of these tanks there are seven large ones and a number of smaller ones—holding in all fifteen thousand to twenty thousand gallons when full. The lower tank alone can be reached on horseback, and to reach the next three requires a stiff climb and a cool head. The upper ones can only be reached by ascending, to a height of several hundred feet, the steep gorge to the right. Even then, except in the case of the highest tank, it is necessary to lower oneself down a rope fastened to the rocks above. There is nothing in external appearances to indicate that water can be found here, and the fact of their very existence is almost unknown to most Americans. . ." So it may be seen that in the heat of summer, when springs and wells were at their lowest

Quitobaquito Spring gushes from a hillside near the Devil's Highway and the border with Mexico. The spring, now in Organ Pipe Cactus National Monument, flowed before recorded history.

ebb and evaporation had depleted waterholes and tanks, there might be little or no water. Even those reaching the tanks, if they were in a weakened condition and found the bottom ones dry, might not be able to climb to the higher ones to reach the precious water there.

The desert road came by its name and its infamy during the California gold rush beginning in 1849. Gold seekers from Mexico and Texas, avoiding travel through the territory of the fierce Apaches to the east, poured over the desert route in their attempts to be the first to reach the goldfields. "Many made the dreaded journey to safety," wrote Capt. Galliard, "but others, unused to desert traveling, their insufficient water supply exhausted, realized their peril and pushed on to Las Tinajas Altas. Some perished of thirst by the way, some wandered from the road and never found the water they craved, some reached the tanks but, finding the water all gone and too weak to go farther, laid down and died. Others reached the longed-for spot, but in such a state of exhaustion that, unless water was found at the lower tank, they were too feeble to climb to the next and perished miserably, their horrors aggravated by the thought that the water for want of which they were perishing was but a few yards off, had they but the strength to reach it.

". . . Fifty graves near the foot of the tanks, marked by rough stones piled in the form of a cross, bear mute testimonial. In all, four hundred persons are said to have perished of thirst between Altar (in Mexico) and Yuma in eight years, and . . . the writer counted sixty-five graves in a single day's ride of a little over thirty miles. So fearful was the death toll that travel along this route soon ceased, and at the time of the survey the road had not been traveled by a vehicle in sixteen years. . ." But though the gold fever had subsided and with it much of the travel over 'the Devil's highway,' it never ceased entirely.

"One of the best known and most pathetic cases of death from thirst," continued Galliard, "was that of an entire Mexican family of six or eight persons. They were pushing on toward Las Tinajas Altas, their total water supply contained in a wicker-covered glass demijohn. When about eight miles from the tanks their horses gave out, and in unloading the wagon by some unfortunate accident their demijohn was broken. Utterly ignorant of the distance to the tanks or of their location, the husband set out alone on foot to find them. Weak and faint, he returned from his unsuccessful search and joined his dying family, where their bodies were all found by the next traveler and buried in a single grave beside the road.

"Pious hands had piled stones on the grave in the form of a cross, and had encircled the whole by a ring, about thirty feet in diameter, of stones piled side by side. This portion of the desert is covered with a thin, stiff crust, which resists the action of the wind but through which wheels easily break. As there is not sufficient rain to obliterate these tracks and nothing else to destroy them, they remain visible for an incredible time. The wagon tracks made when the poor Mexican drove his exhausted team to one side of the road were plainly visible thirty years afterward, and at the very spot still remained pieces of glass and wickerwork from the broken demijohn, and the skulls of the two horses.

"Another equally pathetic case is that of three prospectors who, exhausted for want of water, reached the lower tank only to find that some travelers, who had preceded them only a day or two, had emptied this tank. Feeling sure there was water in the next tank above, they made strenuous efforts to climb to it but were too weak to succeed. They perished at the foot of the almost vertical slope leading to the second tank, where their bodies were found a few days later, the fingers worn to the bone in their dying efforts to reach the water, which was found in abundance in the tank they had tried so hard to reach. . ."

Galliard mentioned some incidents with slightly happier endings, one reported by an army lieutenant in 1855. "On our way to Yuma we met many emigrants returning from California, men and animals suffering from scarcity of water. Some men had died from thirst and others were nearly exhausted. Among those we passed between the Colorado and the Tinajas Altas was a party composed of one woman and three men, on foot, a pack horse in wretched condition carrying their all. The men had given up from pure exhaustion and laid down to die, but the woman, animated by love and sympathy, had plodded on over the long road until she reached water. Clambering up the side of the mountain to the highest (tank), she filled her bota, a sort of leathern flask and, scarcely stopping to rest, started back to resuscitate her dying companions. When we met them she was striding along in advance of the men, animating them by her example.

"Narrower still was the escape of a party of seventeen men and one woman who, overcome by thirst, had laid down to die . . . about twenty-five miles east of the Tinajas Altas. Unwilling to meet death so passively, one man staggered on in the feeble hope of reaching the tanks. In the middle of the night, still eight miles from them, he was found lying insensible beside the road by a veteran traveler, Don Pedro Aguirre of Buenos Ayres (a ranch in southern Arizona). He was on his way with two wagons laden with supplies and water from Yuma to Altar.

"In a few moments the man was stripped and wrapped in a wet blanket, while water was slowly dripped into his mouth with a teaspoon. . . It was evident that he must have had companions, and every effort was made to revive him sufficiently to tell where they (were). Putting him in a wagon, they pressed on with all speed, and just before daylight found his

Pool formed by run-off from Quitobaquito Spring, ringed by desert growth, is only a few yards from the border with Mexico.

seventeen companions, all divested of their clothing, lying alongside the road in the agonies of thirst. To treat properly so large a number sorely taxed the resources of the rescuers but after several hours of hard work the entire party was revived. They and their animals were provided with water and started on their way, blessing Don Pedro and their stout-hearted companion. . ."

Galliard also described other phenomena peculiar to the desert, the sandstorms and mirages. Sandstorms, he said, were more dreaded for the discomforts they caused than any danger to life. "On the Colorado desert where they were most frequent and violent," he wrote, "the first appearance was that of a pale brownish-yellow haze, or cloud, extending many hundred feet above the earth. In the clear atmosphere of the desert this cloud was often visible for hours before it reached the observer, continually increasing in apparent height and density. When the storm had developed its full fury it became about as dark as on a very cloudy or foggy winter's day. The air was full of sand which filled every crevice, crack and cranny of the tent and its furniture, sifted down the backs and into the hair, nostrils, eyes, and clothing of the occupants, accumulated in large quantities in any food which a cook might endeavor to prepare, and cruelly cut the unprotected faces and hands of those exposed to the full fury of the blast.

"Sometimes these storms last but an hour or two, but generally they begin soon after sunrise and last until a little after sunset, but on one occasion quite a severe storm lasted for three entire days. . . One of the greatest dangers to travelers is (the danger of getting) lost, should they attempt to pursue their way while the storm is raging, as it obliterates sandy roads and trails almost as effectually as does snow. When in doubt as to his surroundings and not too short of water, the experienced traveler will generally stop where he is and wait for the storm to cease."

A type of mirage Galliard described was the familiar lake-effect mirage. "At times the water seems very near, not more than two or three hundred yards away; again it appears a mile or two distant. In it trees, shrubs, hills and mountains are reflected exactly as in water, on its surface ripples play, . . . wading near its shore cattle and horses are seen. This form of mirage is peculiar to the bare, flat, and sandy areas of the desert, where the line of sight passes close to the ground. It is most frequent toward the middle of the day when the heat is greatest. . ."

A sizeable region on the Sonoran Desert, east of the harshly rigorous portion traversed by "the Devil's highway" is occupied by a remarkable tribe of desert dwellers, the Papago Indians. These hardy people have always found a homeland in the desert of the southwest United States and northern Mexico. Their lands in this country are now a reservation, the last to be granted to any tribe (in 1916), and the second largest in area. Thus, in all of Arizona's territorial years it was open to American settlement, but there was little, merely a few mines and ranches. The word "Papago" means "bean eaters," and truly the mesquite bean and screwbean, growing wild, were items in their diet. Recently the tribal government announced that the tribe will call itself the Tohono O'odham, their name for themselves in their native Piman tongue. To their great credit, the Indians did not demand that everyone change every reference from "Papagos" to the new name or be branded a racist bigot. So the name "Papago" to designate streets, parks, and other locations in their recognition continues to be used.

Capt. Galliard's writings about the Papago were full of praise for them. "They are the true Arabs of the desert," he wrote, "noted for their strength, fleetness, and endurance, as they must be to carry on successfully the struggle for existence in so inhospitable an area." Wherever there was permanent water, the Papagos set up their villages, mostly of adobes or grass and reed huts similar to wickiups. There they lived during the milder months of the year, but in the extreme heat of summer they would move to outdoor ramadas as dwellings. Sometimes complete villages would be entirely vacant for months on end, standing silently, waiting to be re-occupied.

"Like all inhabitants of the desert," Galliard went on, "they are . . . a pastoral people, owning herds of fine cattle, and tough, wiry ponies. They are, however, excellent runners and will cover on foot, in a day, a distance few horsemen would under-take. . . . At many places, where fertile land can be found near natural waterholes or convenient to their artificially-constructed dams, they establish temporary homes . . . When the first summer rain falls, where silence reigned all is full of life and activity. . . Often within twenty-four hours after the first drop of rain falls, the entire crop of melons, pumpkins, squashes, beans and Indian corn have been planted. . ."

An absorbing account of life and death on the desert was left by Charlie Eastman, a noted Arizona pioneer. He left California for Sonora, Mexico, in 1883. There, he said, he "drove cattle and fought Indians." He traveled to Tombstone, and from there to the Quijotoa gold mine and the Vekol silver mine on the desert south of Casa Grande. Arriving in Casa Grande in 1884, he took up a ranch in the valley south of the town, and now part of the Papago reservation. "With the flood waters from Cockleburr Wash," he said, "I raised everything, but lost my cattle in the drought of 1916 and quit ranching.

"I have known men to go a hundred miles on only a gallon of water—done it myself," said Eastman in his reminiscences, "and I have known others just as strong physically who have tried to go fifty miles with plenty of water only to become exhausted and perish if not rescued in time. It depends on whether you get rattled and excited or keep your head clear. I learned from the wisdom of an old Papago I was traveling with over the hot desert, and his advice perhaps saved my life on one occasion. He told me when you are thirsty and don't have too much water to take a mouthful out of your canteen, hold it in your mouth about five minutes, gargle with it as it cools your favored insides, then spit it out, and you will not crave half as much water.

"I learned on my own not to start out on the desert after a big spree, as the alcoholic drinks would aggravate the thirst on the hot desert. I remember an Irishman working on the Quijotoa mine, in the early '80s, got on a jamboree and was canned the next day. He started for the Gunsight Mine, thirty miles to the west where his brother was working. The Indians found his bones scattered in the desert afterwards. He did not have but a gallon canteen of water when he left camp. There was a road leading from Quijotoa to Gunsight, but the Irishman (tried) to shorten the distance by cutting across the hot desert and got hopelessly lost. Walking, walking and getting nowhere consumed all his energy, and he perished.

"In the early '90s I walked from Casa Grande to Gunsight Mine, a distance of over ninety miles. My brother-in-law, Fred Wall, who had charge of some gold properties . . . wrote me to come and go to work. As there was no travel on the road between Casa Grande and Gunsight, that mine having shut down some years previously, and as there was but one place where there was water on the road, I concluded to use a burro to pack my blankets, grub and water for the trip.

"While preparing for the journey a strapping young fellow from the east named Bob Cooper elected to go with me. He said he hitch-hiked across the continent to Arizona, was broke, and had to land work somewhere. I tried to discourage him, tried to impress him with the fact we had to cross a waterless desert in the hottest time of the year (June), that we might not meet a soul except some Indians, but with all this admonishment he still insisted on going. Little did Bob Cooper dream that he was going on his last journey.

"The second day out in the morning the burro bolted with

our blankets, food and spare water, so all we had was a half gallon of water apiece and a can of tomatoes that dropped out of the pack—a kind of slim sustenance to walk on in the broiling sun for about sixty miles. The only solution to the problem I could see, and I told the tenderfoot so, was to rest in the shade of some mesquite tree during the hottest time of the day and do our walking in the cool evenings and the moonlit night when we could see the road. I forgot that the rattlesnakes liked being in the soft, fine sand of the road in the evening after the sand had cooled off; consequently we had to give up the idea of traveling at night.

"The only thing that saved us, being without water so far (the tenderfoot having finished his and most of mine), was the can of tomatoes. When resting in the middle of the day under some shade tree I would cut the can open, let the little breeze there was cool the top layers of the tomatoes off, and by eating them quench our thirst. The fourth day, when only one mile from the Gunsight Well (the well was in a ravine and could not be seen until on the top of it), Cooper got delirious—plumb crazy—pulled his clothes off, even his shoes, and started over a rock-strewn mesa toward a high mountain in his stocking feet, hollering to me he could see water on top of the mountain. When he saw I didn't pay any attention to him, he turned around and came running after me.

"About that time I had got to the well where my brother-in-law and George Sayers were pumping water to the Gunsight Mine through a pipe six miles long, and as Cooper got there they promptly knocked him down and tied him up so he couldn't jump into the well. They gave him strong black coffee with little sips of water in between. After a few days Cooper was partly restored and his faculties clear. He admitted that the desert with its trackless wastes and mocking heat mirages had tricked him, that he was unaccustomed to such hardships, and that the struggle of walking through fine, loose sand in the road, stumbling into and out of rock-strewn gullies in the scorching sun was not what it was cracked up to be. It was even a torture to the desert bred.

"He made up his mind to go into Gila Bend with the first team that went there, and wire his folks for money to go back east to his home where he could have the satisfaction of croaking between clean sheets. Poor fellow. Going to Gila Bend with a freight team the sun got another crack at him, with the result that he died in the street in town as he got off the wagon. The coroner's jury verdict was 'dead of heat prostration.' I will never forget the sight of Bob Cooper laying at the well, tied up, a dust-caked, sun-scorched figure who couldn't talk through cracking lips and swollen tongue. Lord spare me not to see another one like it."

While Eastman was farming south of Maricopa, the body of a man was found near his farm. Crazed by thirst, he had cut his own throat. Not long after this tragedy, Eastman was cutting hay when a man approached him from the direction of Maricopa where there was a railroad way station. The man was wearing a long black overcoat, in hot weather. In broken English, he asked Eastman for some water and something to eat. He explained that he was a Catholic priest who had been "run out of" Chihuahua, a state in northern Mexico, and was on his way to Lower California where he had French relatives and friends. "After having his fill of grub and water," Eastman continued, "I told him he had a long tramp ahead of him over a hot, waterless desert, and suggested it would be better for him to go back to Maricopa and follow the railroad track. He told me the reason he would not do that was that he had some gold and silver ornaments belonging to the church on his person, and was afraid some tramp would rob him. I guess he told the truth, because he wanted to pay me with some kind of ornament, half gold and half silver, used by Catholics in the baptism service.

"I wouldn't accept it. 'Father,' I told him, 'you are always welcome to stay on an Arizona cattle ranch as long as you want to and it won't cost you a cent. But with all due respect to your chosen profession, you are going to take a gallon canteen of water with you (he only had a quart bottle of water when he came) and some lunch, whether you go on south or back to Maricopa. I am getting mighty tired of hauling fly-blown Frenchmen out of the desert, as I lugged one out a short time ago,' referring to the fellow with his throat cut."

Charlie Eastman, who loved yet feared and respected the Sonoran Desert, ended his reminiscences with a unique soliloquy: "Some people, such as Bob Cooper and the French padre, never think of starvation, lingering death, or the swifter horrors of death by thirst when they are cut off from civilization and dropped into the desert. The old desert rat prospector—he is calm, philosophical, has lost all dread and fear of the unknown, has the courage and daring to overcome every obstacle that comes his way. The desert has many mysteries and tragedies, some of which are solved, others never. I have known a few men who started out across the desert and vanished completely, never to be heard from again and not a trace of them being found. Mother Nature intended that man should conquer the desert, because she gave it the lure that holds men forever, she scattered waterholes about, and at times makes the desert bloom with sweetly-scented wild flowers."

Chapter 10

Clifton, As Tough As They Came

Arizona in the latter half of the 1800s was truly the wild west, most of the towns springing up in that period having their raucous day in the sun. The town's remoteness, or distance from any established rule of law, contributed to how wild it would become and for how long. So when the boom came to Clifton, in the remoteness of Arizona's southeast near the New Mexico border, all of the conditions were ripe for one of the wildest towns Arizona and the Southwest ever saw.

In 1870 the fearsome Chiricahua Apache Indians dominated the region, part of their homeland in which they held absolute sway despite the efforts of soldiers sent to subdue them. The great chief Cochise had declared implacable war against the whites after an incident in 1861 in Apache Pass. There he had been tricked by a green lieutenant just out of West Point, several of his relatives were taken prisoner, and four of his male relatives were hanged by the soldiers before they returned to their post. Cochise swore vengeance, and after almost ten years was still on the warpath. It would be another two years before he consented to a peace treaty.

Depredations along the Arizona-New Mexico border by Apaches led a Captain Chase to pursue them westward from Silver City, New Mexico, just across the Arizona border. Chase hired a Civil War veteran, Bob Metcalf, and his brother Jim as scouts for his company. In time they reached the San Francisco River in Arizona, and a tributary they named Chase Creek in honor of their captain. While scouting the Indians, Bob Metcalf took notice of the outcroppings of copper ores in that area. After the treaty with Cochise was signed in 1872, Bob Metcalf and his brother returned to investigate the copper indications they had discovered.

View of Chase Creek with smelter stack in background. "Little Emma" would travel from track on far side to the Longfellow Mine incline. (Courtesy Greenlee County Historical Society)

In 1873 the Metcalfs had located the Metcalf and Longfellow mining claims, and were followed by other prospectors who filed on more claims. Near the spot that Chase Creek flowed into the San Francisco River under the towering cliffs, a town began gradually to grow, known as Cliff Town which in time became Clifton. It was still part of one of Arizona's four original counties, Yavapai, the county seat of which was more than two hundred miles away. The prospectors got together and formed the Copper Mountain Mining District. Doing it that way, they would not have to go all the way to Prescott to file their claims.

Clifton at first was the site only of a general store and a primitive adobe smelter. The country was so wild and remote, with only primitive trails and wagon roads connecting it with the outside world, that transporting the ore out for processing was prohibitively expensive. The adobe furnaces, fired by charcoal, worked to a degree but were prone to "freeze up," suddenly lose their intense heat. Then the unrefined copper lump in the smelter, called a "sow," became useless, too heavy to transport and too expensive to bother with as there was so much ore. These sows were buried on the spot, another furnace constructed, and operations resumed.

A narrow gauge railcar track was built down the incline from the Longfellow mine more than five miles to the smelter. The ore cars moved by gravity, and with the ore also carried teams of mules, which were hitched to the emptied cars to haul them back up the incline. This system worked until 1879, when a small locomotive was shipped by rail to La Junta, Colorado. There it was disassembled and the parts freighted all the way to Clifton to be reassembled. The engine was dubbed "Little Emma," the assembly done by a railroad man named Henry "Dad" Arbuckle. He became the locomotive's engineer, and it gave great service for many years.

For some years Clifton grew slowly. Investors with names like Shannon, Underwood and Lezinsky struggled to make the mines paying operations. Then in 1883 a corporation was organized in Scotland, the Arizona Copper Co., Ltd., bought some of the best mines, formed a development group, and Clifton and its mines were finally on the way. Construction work began on a railroad from Lordsburg to Clifton, plenty of payroll money was flowing, attracting the gamblers, saloon

"Little Emma," the small locomotive that hauled ore cars in Clifton's early days. Assembled and engineered by Henry "Dad" Arbuckle, it was finally retired and put on display seen here. (Courtesy Greenlee County Historical Society.)

keepers, and others of the "sporting crowd" to Clifton. After ten years it had become a full-blown wild-west town, wide open twenty-four hours a day, where shootings and knifings were common.

The site of the old adobe smelter was to be cleared for the erection of a new, modern mill and smelter, so an economic benefit at once was realized. Sam Lezinsky, foreman of the old smelter crew, made an offer to dig up the old sows, chunks of almost pure copper, to run through the new mill. He obtained a contract from the Scotch company, under which he would receive four-and-a-half cents a pound for the copper he recovered, provided he delivered it in chunks not over twelve-inch cubes for convenience in running through the new smelter. This proved to be the biggest obstacle of the salvage job. The sows could not be drilled for blasting, except where a natural seam might occur. Lezinsky designed some special equipment. Large cutters were forged, held by one man, while two others swinging twelve-pound sledgehammers struck the cutter. This went on for several months, but in the end all of the sows were recovered at a handsome profit for Lezinsky and his crew.

In the meantime Clifton was booming along. Chase Creek Street was lined along both sides with saloons, gambling halls and bawdy houses. In the Chinese quarter opium dens flourished. It was said by someone that every vice known to man could be satisfied on Chase Creek Street. Along with them were the "respectable" businesses, stores of every kind, and the offices of professional men, doctors, lawyers, and assayers. The town was cut in half by the stream flowing at the foot of Chase Creek Street, but the problem it caused was overcome by the installation of a swinging foot bridge over it for pedestrians, though the stream still had to be forded by all other transportation.

For a time Clifton had to bear the domination of the town by a gang that stole, robbed, and beat and murdered people at will and unrestrained. The gang members were Red Sample, Tex Yorkey, Dan Dowd, Bill Delaney, Jim Howard and John Heath. One of their tricks was to surprise a businessman in his store after hours, demand that he open the safe and give them the money, and beat him into insensibility if he refused. One victim was William Church, superintendent of the Detroit Copper

Clifton's main street, Chase Creek, in about 1910, looking east (though caption says "looking south." (Courtesy Greenlee County Historical Society)

Company a few miles downriver from Clifton. When Church refused their demands, they beat him over the head with their six-guns until in desperation he gave them the combination, whereupon they opened the safe and took its contents. They repeated the caper with store owners Jim Yankee and Leonce Frasinette, and kept this up for months even though everyone in town knew their identities, including the sheriff's deputies.

One of those who went to Clifton to get in on the ground floor of the new prosperity was John Hovey, who opened a big frame dance hall and saloon. He hired as his major domo a former legislator and superintendent of one of the Lezinsky-owned mines, John McCormack. Hovey's place immediately became immensely popular, as he was the jovial sort and McCormack was well liked by everybody in town. For about four years the place never closed, day or night, and McCormack made Hovey a mint of money until one night he was killed by a Mexican tinhorn gambler named Alvino Aguirre.

After drinking and gambling all day, Aguirre lost his last dollar at about three in the morning at a faro table. He looked up McCormack, told him that he had lost all his money and wanted to borrow twenty dollars to try to recoup. He said he had some money at his home, and that if he lost the twenty he would go home, get the money, and repay McCormack yet that night. McCormack agreed on those terms, but cautioned Aguirre, "You must pay it back tonight, as it is house money, and I must have it when I make up the day's receipts," and loaned Aguirre the twenty dollars.

Aguirre went back to the faro table where his luck turned, and he won a wad of cash. He left Hovey's and went to another gambling hall. When he had not returned to repay the loan, McCormack went to his room and to bed. Aguirre danced, drank and gambled all night and all the next day until late in the afternoon when he again went broke. He went home and got the money he had there, went back to the gambling house, and lost every cent of that, too.

When McCormack went on duty at Hovey's that evening, Aguirre was standing at the bar. McCormack called him over. "Where's the twenty you borrowed?" he asked. "When you didn't come back and pay it, like you promised, I had to make it up out of my own pocket. I don't like that way of doing, and your word's not good with me anymore." At that Alvino pulled his six-gun. "You calling me a liar?" he grated, and threw down on McCormack who was behind the bar. McCormack put his hands on the bar and vaulted over it intending to grapple with Aguirre, but Aguirre fired striking McCormack in the groin. He fell to the floor, groaning, "He's got me, boys."

A bystander grabbed Aguirre's gun and, taking a full swing, bashed him on the head with it. The gun exploded, and Aguirre went down bleeding profusely at the head. Everyone thought he had been shot in the head and was a goner, but it was later found that his gun was a single-action model that he must have cocked again after shooting McCormack. It was like that when it was twisted out of his hand, and he was knocked out by the ramrod or extractor protruding from the gun. It was this cut that bled so profusely, the bullet smashed into the bar, and Aguirre was not killed.

McCormack was carried to his room; a small, blue hole was found in his groin where the bullet took effect, but it was not bleeding. He was told that the wound was probably a bad one and that he was bleeding internally. The wounded man sent for Hovey, and two letters were written for him before he collapsed.

When he was revived he and Hovey talked over some business matters, and saying, "Good-bye, boys, I'm gone," McCormack sank into a coma again. He never regained consciousness and died about three hours later.

At McCormack's death, Hovey searched the town for Aguirre, including every Mexican hovel. No sign of Aguirre was found, his friends probably having spirited him away and hidden him or rushed him out of town. McCormack was buried the next day, and practically the whole Anglo population in town attended the funeral. Upon Hovey's return from the cemetery he summoned a sign painter, and had him paint a sign on the back bar mirror: "One Thousand Dollars Reward for Alvino Aguirre, Dead or Alive. Jno. H. Hovey." It was called to everyone's attention, Hovey hoping it would tempt someone who knew something to tell it.

About six weeks later, Hovey told his new manager that he was going to Solomonville, the county seat, on business and left on horseback that day. A few days later, the manager received a note from Hovey saying he would be gone a few days longer, as he was going to look at some gold properties down near the Mexican border. About ten days later Hovey returned, his horse showing evidence of being ridden hard and Hovey himself of extreme fatigue.

Hovey gave his horse to a hostler to care for, walked into the saloon, and summoned some of the bystanders to come and have a drink with him. He then stuck a cigar (which he seldom lighted) in his mouth and chewed on it as he took a stool to the bar mirror, dipped a towel in the water, and washed off the reward notice on the mirror. Instructing the bartender to clean up the mirror, Hovey crossed the room and sat down in a lookout's chair at a faro table.

One of Hovey's best friends, Ben Crawford, came in later in the day. Seeing the sign missing, he asked Hovey if he had given up on Aguirre. Hovey said that Aguirre had died in Sonora, Mexico. "Are you sure, John?" asked Crawford. "Yes, I'm sure," replied Hovey. "He died down there about ten days ago. I saw his grave." Hovey had, of course, learned of Aguirre's location in Solomonville, had ridden into Mexico alone, and killed the man who murdered his friend.

Clifton's main street, Chase Creek, in about 1910, looking west (though caption says "looking north." (Courtesy Greenlee County Historical Society)

One of Arizona's noted pioneers, Charles M. "Charley" Clark, arrived in Clifton in 1883. Clark had been the first telegraph operator in the territory, arriving at Maricopa Wells in 1873 to become the first military operator. In Clifton he went to work for Jake Abraham who had just completed the Clifton Hotel. Clark was the telegraph operator and was also night clerk for the hotel. Space was at such a premium that the hotel and telegraph office was in the hotel's hallway, and Abraham had had to build a long board-and-batten annex in the back with a canvas roof. This annex was familiarly known as "telephone row," because a word spoken at one end of the room could be distinctly heard at the other.

In the annex were sixty-four canvas cots. They were rented at one dollar per night. Clark's duties as clerk were to collect the rentals and pilot the drunks to their proper cots. When they were all full, he placed the "S.R.O." sign over the desk and was free to retire himself. The hotel register and safe were also in the hallway with the desk. Since considerable money would accumulate, Clark had asked Abraham not to leave any in the safe overnight. He told him that if the gang came after him, he would give them the key to the safe rather than take a beating. Abraham, however, was adamant that they would never rob his place, and they never did.

Of all the members of the gang operating in Clifton at the time, John Heath was the only one with an honest income. He opened and successfully ran a saloon and gambling hall. Occasionally Heath would go on a bender for days at a time, during which he never went near his own place of business but drank and gambled at his competitors' places of business. He was a faro addict and spent much time at the tables. Whenever during his sprees of drinking and gambling he chanced to run out of money, he would simply borrow from anyone who was handy and would lend him cash, until he became exhausted physically and financially.

Charley Clark was well acquainted with Heath, and on friendly terms, thinking it to be unwise and unhealthy to be otherwise. Heath had borrowed from Clark on a few occasions, twenty or thirty dollars at a time, which was always promptly repaid when Heath sobered up.

One night at about midnight Clark had just bedded down the last drunk on "telephone row" and gone back to the hotel office in the hall. He made up the cash for the day, preparing to retire to his own room. He tossed the cash pouch into the safe and was about to give the combination a whirl, when Heath came in alone. The outlaw dropped a hand on his gun butt as he said, "Clark, howdy." Clark was sure that his turn to be robbed had come, as Heath was carrying two beautiful, ivory-handled six-guns in his holsters. Heath, however, approached the desk and said, "Clark, I want to borrow thirty dollars."

Greatly relieved, Clark reached into his pocket and brought out what money he had, which was only twenty-two dollars. He offered it to Heath, saying it was all he had but Heath was welcome to it. Heath, however, replied that he could have gotten the money at his own place, but that he was going out of town for a few days and didn't want anyone, especially those in his saloon, to know that he was going away. He asked Charley if there wasn't some way he could make up the other eight dollars. Clark finally took the eight dollars from the house money, and put in his own IOU.

Heath wadded up the money and stuck it into his pocket. "I'm mighty grateful, Clark," he said, "and I won't forget to return it." He then took one of the Colt .45 revolvers from its holster and slid it over to Clark. It was worth sixty to seventy-five dollars at the time. As he started out the door, Clark called to him. "Here, John," he said, "you have left one of your guns." Heath replied, "That's all right, I've got another one." Clark said, "But you're going out, and will need both of your guns. I've loaned you money before and never asked for security, have I?"

"No, but this is different," Heath told him. "I'm going away, and if I don't come back I don't want you to be a loser because of me." Clark persisted, "What's the matter with you? Take your gun; you'll be walking sideways without it." "No," said Heath, "you keep it until I get back, and if I don't never call for it, the gun is yours." And he walked out the door.

Going down to Hovey's dance hall, Heath spied the man he was looking for, at a table playing stud poker. Heath jerked his gun and fired, and the man fell over with his head bleeding profusely. Heath covered the crowd with his gun and backed out of the dance hall, sprang upon his horse and galloped out of

Funeral procession lining up on Chase Creek street in Clifton in front of Sacred Heart Catholic Church, the first building on the left. (Courtesy Greenlee County Historical Society)

town certain that he had killed his man. The victim was carried to another room, laid out on a table, and the doctor summoned. Then it was found that the lower part of his left ear was shot off but that was the only damage. The doctor bound up his wound with adhesive tape, and soon the shootee was back playing stud poker, apparently not much the worse for wear.

Word eventually got back to Heath in hiding, through his friends, that the man he had shot was not killed, and in about a week he ventured to drift back into Clifton. He went to the hotel that night, handed thirty dollars to Clark, and said, "I guess I'll take Betsy out of hock, and I'm sure obliged to you." Clark handed him back his gun, saying, "John, I've seen you shoot, and I sure thought you were a better shot than that." "I am a good shot," Heath told him, "and if that sucker had not chose just that moment to look at his hole card, I'd a got him." The poker player had ducked his head to peek at his hole card just as Heath fired, the movement of his head just enough to get it in the ear rather than in the middle of his head.

The Clifton gang, Delaney, Dowd, Heath, Howard, Kelley (or Yorkey), and Sample in due time got what was coming to them, though it wasn't in Clifton. The two deputy sheriffs in town, each of whom ran a prosperous saloon on his own, had maintained a rather cool relationship, each thinking the other was in cahoots with the outlaws. When they finally got together and discovered that neither was cozy with the outlaws and both wanted badly to rid the town of them, they contacted some prominent citizens and made sure they were solidly on the side of the law. Then the outlaw gang was emphatically told that its company was no longer desired in Clifton and they had better get out of town pronto. The gang turned up in Bisbee on December 8, 1883, where they tried to open the game by resorting to their old tactics.

Heath had scouted around town for a few days, staying in the background, and on his advice the five remaining gang members rode into Bisbee and up to Goldwater and Casteneda's store, one of the town's prominent mercantile houses. Kelley was left to hold the horses, Dowd and Delaney were detailed to guard duty in the street, while Howard and Sample entered the store. Unobtrusively they made their way to the living quarters

John Heath was lynched by a Bisbee mob and hanged from a telephone pole in Tombstone, on February 22, 1884. (Arizona Historic Photos)

in the rear of the store, where J. M. Castaneda, an old man, lay ill. He tried to resist, but the outlaws gave him a beating and forced him to hand over the money hidden in the back.

Then Howard and Sample went into the store itself, got the drop on the customers, and ordered Julius Goldwater to open the safe. As they were backing out of the store, covering those inside with their guns, shooting broke out in the street. Someone had discovered that a robbery was in progress, and fired at one of the lookouts. Dowd, Delaney, Kelley and Sample shot their way out of it, leaving four citizens dead in the streets, including a woman. Only one of the bandits was slightly scratched.

There was a tremendous uproar in Bisbee as a result. The woman's death especially enraged the town, as she had been particularly loved and respected by everyone, and three men had been brutally murdered. The outlaws had fled into the

Sulphur Springs Valley headed east toward the Chiricahua Mountains, and several posses took the trail after them. The first posse to leave town was in command of a deputy sheriff, and included a man named John Heath. No one knew he was one of the gang.

Loudly denouncing the perpetrators of this foul deed, Heath managed to steer the posse into following a false trail, thereby losing several valuable hours' time. The robbers made it into the mountains and promptly scattered. The deputy sheriff became suspicious of Heath and his actions, and put him under arrest until the lawman could check him out. Heath was soon identified by a lumber hauler as the man he had seen in the company of the outlaws the day before the robbery and killing spree, and was tossed into the calaboose to wait while the others were rounded up.

Dowd was caught in Chihuahua, Old Mexico, and Delaney in Sonora. Both were sneaked back across the border by cooperative Mexican rurales without benefit of extradition. Kelly was tripped up in Deming, New Mexico, after arguing with a barber and refusing to pay him. Howard and Sample were arrested near Clifton, Howard after giving a watch to a dance-hall girl whose jealous boyfriend recognized it and tipped off the authorities. They all went to trial, including Heath, in February, 1884, in the county courthouse in Tombstone. Charged with robbery and murder, all were found guilty, Heath was sentenced to life imprisonment, and the rest to be hanged.

The hanging sentences were just what the citizens of Bisbee wanted, but Heath's life term did not set well at all. A secret mass meeting was held and a vigilante committee appointed to take care of the situation. One night forty to fifty men secretly took the road to Tombstone, and suddenly in the pre-dawn darkness of February 22, 1884, they stormed the county jail. Only Heath was taken from his cell. At the edge of town he was hanged from a telephone pole, and the vigilantes rode back to Bisbee unchallenged.

The people of Tombstone, having seen enough of outlaws themselves, were entirely sympathetic. A coroner's jury was summoned to examine Heath's body and fix the cause of death. Its verdict: "We find the deceased came to his death as the result of emphysema of the lungs, probably, and possibly induced by strangulation." Not long thereafter scaffolding was put up in the courtyard of the Tombstone county courthouse, and on March 28, 1884, the remaining five gang members were legally hanged and buried in Boothill Cemetery.

To return to the fortunes of Clifton, however, Charley Clark had been appointed to the offices of postmaster and justice of the peace, by the county supervisors, when his predecessor resigned. Though the gang was gone, that detracted nothing from the rip-roaring, wide-open Clifton where the gin-mills and other houses of pleasure never closed, and shootings, holdups and cuttings were commonplace. A cowboy who Clark called "Charley Strong" came to town where he fell ill with typhoid fever. He took a room in the Clifton Hotel where Clark was night clerk, and holed up there for the disease to run its course.

In a few weeks he felt recovered enough to walk down to Hovey's dance hall, about four blocks away, to meet some of his cowboy buddies in off the range. The exertion and drinking proved to be too much in his weakened condition, and he had to tell his friends farewell and that he had to go back to his room. As he left, two Mexicans accosted him. One said, "Would you like to go to my room? I have a good bed and plenty of blankets and you will be comfortable." The other urged him to go to "Juan's room." Strong told them thanks, but no thanks, he wanted to go to his own room where his clothing and medicine were, and lie down there.

About half a block from the hotel was the post office, where Clark was making out a money order report. He was startled by two shots just outside his window, and heard the sound of running footsteps of a man going up the sidewalk to the hotel. Clark grabbed his gun, blew out the lamp, and ran outside just in time to see a man run into an alley past the side of the hotel to a passageway behind the buildings in that block. In the street were two Mexicans, very dead, not moving or making a sound.

A constable, gun in hand, came running up. Clark told him to go down to Louie Abrams' saloon, and that in the card room in the back he would find a man breathing hard from running. The constable was to hold that man there until Clark could get down there to talk to him. The coroner was summoned, and he and Clark found that the two Mexicans were both dead from gunshots to the head, that one had a knife in his hand, and that the other had his hand on his knife which was at his belt. Leaving the coroner to supervise the removal of the bodies, Clark went to Abrams' saloon, to the card room in the back, and there found the constable, Johnson, talking to cowboy Charley Strong.

Clark told the constable to leave the room, as he wanted to talk to Strong alone, and not to permit anyone to enter the room until he had finished his examination. When Johnson was gone, Clark asked Strong why he had killed the two Mexicans. Asked if they were both dead, Clark said they were, and Strong replied, "I'm glad they are. Look what they did to me," raising his right arm and showing where his coat was slashed from the shoulder almost to the wrist. "I half expected something like what happened," he said, "and I was partly prepared." The point of the knife had evidently just touched him, as he was scratched and bleeding all along his arm where the clothing was cut.

Clark took out his pocketknife, placed his thumb about half an inch from the point, jabbed into Strong's shoulder, and drew it down his arm, slashing him the full length of the cut in his clothing. The startled cowboy began to threaten Clark, as he bled profusely from the deep cut, but Clark told him to keep quiet. He summoned Johnson, told him Strong was bleeding to death, and sent him out for all the hot water he could find. He came back with plenty of it. Strong was stripped of his shirt, which was torn into bandages, and the arm was tightly bound after it was washed with the hot water.

Clark sent Johnson for a doctor, and the three helped the cowboy to his room, where the doctor re-dressed the wound, binding the edges together with adhesive tape. Strong was put under house arrest, in the charge of the proprietor of the hotel, and he made a rapid recovery of both his fever and the cut on his arm. The district attorney came up from the county seat at Solomonville for Strong's hearing. His bloody coat and the remains of his shirt were entered into evidence as Exhibits A and B, and he was bound over to the next term of court in custody of the sheriff. There he entered a plea of self-defense, and was acquitted forthwith.

Twelve years later, Clark was in Jerome, where he had moved, and where there had been a disastrous fire in the business district. He was walking among the still smoldering ruins of the business building he had owned, wondering how he would get back on his feet. A man approached him, and asked if he was Judge Clark, justice of the peace in Clifton twelve years previously. Clark replied affirmatively. "You don't recognize me, do you?" inquired the man. Clark said no, he didn't though he looked familiar. The man said that he was Charley Strong, now married, with a family and the owner of a stock ranch.

"I've just sold a shipment of cattle," he said, "and have $16,000 sitting in the bank I'm not using. I want you to take that money and use it to get yourself back on your feet. You can repay me anytime." Stunned, Clark was taken aback. But he answered "no," he appreciated the offer, but could not assure he could ever pay it back. So the two men talked over old times, had a drink, and said good-bye again.

Clifton was also the home for a time of two of the most legendary characters ever to inhabit Arizona. One was named Rufus Nephews, born in Washington, D. C., but he had drifted west to become a cowboy with the famed Hash Knife outfit. He used so much Climax chewing tobacco that he came to be called "Climax Jim," and his primary trade came to be dealing in other people's cattle. As a business necessity he became an expert at lock picking, specializing in jail doors, leg irons and handcuffs. It came to the situation that any time there was a crime with no evidence of forcible entry, Climax Jim was the number one suspect.

Once Climax Jim was caught rustling cattle in Graham County, tossed in the pokey and held for trial. In court he produced witnesses who testified that the offense occurred not in Graham County, but in Apache County, and Jim was acquitted. Promptly re-arrested, he was charged with stealing the same cattle in Apache County, and taken there for trial. On trial in Apache County, he produced witnesses who swore that the cattle were rustled, not in Apache County, but in Graham County, and he was acquitted again. On another occasion the

Bank of Morenci sent a bunch of cancelled payroll checks back to the Arizona Copper Company, but they never arrived, having been stolen from the post office. Climax Jim was apprehended trying to cash one of them after he had removed the "paid" stamp. At his trial in Solomonville, the district attorney entered the check in evidence as Exhibit A, and carelessly laid it on the table. At a discreet moment, Jim reached over unnoticed, got the check, chewed it up and swallowed it. The government's case was dismissed, gone for lack of evidence.

The other character of reference went under the sobriquet of "Cyclone Bill," though his real name was W. E. "Abe" Beck. In Texas, he had graduated from law school and been admitted to the bar, but turned to cow punching instead. Because of a gunshot wound, one of his legs had grown shorter than the other, and when he stood on the good leg he appeared to be an average-sized man, but when he stood down on the gimpy leg he seemed very short. Unable to do hard physical labor, he had to live by his wits.

Cyclone Bill first came to wide public notice by being suspected, because of his distinctive limp, of being one of the robbers in the famous Wham army payroll robbery. For a while, Bill let the law officers stew, but at length produced an alibi. The robbery occurred on Saturday, May 11, 1889. But a man and wife testified that Cyclone Bill had stopped at their cabin, more than eighty miles from the robbery scene, on Friday, May 10th, and stayed there until Sunday morning when he left for Clifton. At this testimony, Bill was released from custody.

Cyclone Bill once ran for justice of the peace in Clifton against a man named Abe Boyles. Boyles was a fine man, but the sporting crowd of which Cyclone Bill, as a tinhorn gambler, was a member in good standing decided it would provide some humor in an otherwise dull election by running Bill against him. So many people voted for Bill that for a while it seemed that he had won the election. Since he was not a regular nominee, however, his name had to be written in. One ballot was marked Cyclone, one said Tornado Williams, and eleven others Cyclone Bill. This not being his true name, the thirteen ballots were tossed out by the election officials, and Boyles won by three votes.

There was a law on the books then, however, to the effect that any district having more than five thousand voters was entitled to another justice of the peace. Cyclone Bill took his own census, found that there were more than five thousand voters, and set up his own justice court. The county supervisors ruled that Bill's private census was invalid, and Bill had to retire from the bench.

Clifton probably has the distinction of being the only town in Arizona to have been in four counties at one time or other. Originally it was in Yavapai County, one of the state's original four. When in 1879 Apache County was created, Clifton was in the portion of Yavapai County that was chopped off and given to Apache. Graham County was organized in 1881 with Solomonville the county seat, and Clifton was in the portion of Apache County, with some from Pima County, that made up Graham. This was the situation until 1909, when Greenlee County was created out of Graham County with Clifton the county seat of Greenlee as it is today.

If all the pioneers who knew Clifton when it was young were suddenly reincarnated, they would recognize it, as a lot of it is still as it was in the Old West. There is a lot they wouldn't recognize, though. The old mines have come into the hands of a new mining company, and now are worked as a vast open pit mine that has gobbled up all the old underground shafts, obliterated frontier towns and caused highways to be re-routed. At times there is a lot of excitement in the streets, too, because the miners are organized now, and when they go on strike they mean business. Law officers have to be sent to keep the peace, with tense confrontations resulting.

Clifton's residents are still proud of its wild west heritage, after all, and they'll still re-tell for you the old legends. Like the one about Margarito Varela, a Mexican stone mason with a reputation for hard work of a superior quality. He was hired to build Clifton's first jail, which he carved out of the solid rock of a hillside. At its completion he was paid off for his labors and promptly went on a spree, which included shooting up the town, at the conclusion of which he became the first occupant of Clifton's new jail.

Bibliography
& Suggested Reading List

Ahnert, Gerald. Retracing the Butterfield Overland Trail Through Arizona. Los Angeles: Westernlore Press, 1973.

Barnes, Will C. Arizona Place Names. Ed. Byrd Granger. Tucson: University of Arizona Press, 1960.

Bourke, John G. On the Border With Crook. New York: Charles Scribner's Sons, 1891.

Breakenridge, William M. Helldorado. Boston: Houghton-Mifflin, 1928.

Browne, J. Ross. Adventures in the Apache Country. New York: Harper & Bros., 1869.

Burns, Walter N. Tombstone: An Iliad of the Southwest. Garden City, N.Y.: Doubleday, 1929.

Cremony, John C. Life Among the Apaches. New York: A. Roman & Co., 1868.

Cruse, Thomas. Apache Days and After. Caldwell, Idaho: The Caxton Press, 1961.

Falk, Odie B. Arizona: A Short History. Norman, Okla.: University of Oklahoma Press, 1970.

Farish, Thomas. History of Arizona. Phoenix: Flimer Bros., 1915.

Griffith, A. Kinney. Mickey Free, Manhunter. Caldwell, Idaho: Caxton Printers, 1969.

Lake, Stuart. Wyatt Earp, Frontier Marshal. Boston: Houghton-Mifflin, 1931.

Lauer, Charles D. Old West Adventures in Arizona. Phoenix: Golden West Publishers, 1989.

Lauer, Charles D. Tales of Arizona Territory. Phoenix: Golden West Publishers, 1990.

Mazzonovich, Anton. Trailing Geronimo. Los Angeles: Gem Publishing Co., 1926.

Marshall, Otto N. The Wham Paymaster Robbery. Pima, Ariz.: Chamber of Commerce, 1967.

Merrill, W. Earl. One Hundred Yesterdays. Mesa, Ariz.: Privately Published, 1972.

Murbarger, Nell. Ghosts of the Adobe Walls. Los Angeles: Westernlore Press, 1964.

Parker, Stanley W. Southwestern Arizona Ghost Towns. Las Vegas: Nevada Publications, 1981.

Stratton, E. O. Pioneering in Arizona: The Reminiscences of Emerson Oliver Stratton. Ed. John A. Carroll. Tucson: Arizona Historical Society, 1964.

Thrapp, Dan L. The Conquest of Apacheria. Norman, Okla.: University of Oklahoma Press, 1967.

Traywick, Ben T. The Residents of Tombstone's Boot Hill. Privately Published, 1971.

Trimble, Marshall. Arizona Adventure. Phoenix: Golden West Publishers, 1982.

Tuska, John. Billy The Kid. Westport, Conn.: Greenfield Press, 1982.

Various Contributors. A Historical and Biographical Record of the Territory of Arizona. Chicago: McFarland & Poole, 1896.

Zarbin, Earl. The Swilling Legacy. Phoenix: Salt River Project, 1980.

Index

Other Books by Charles D. Lauer

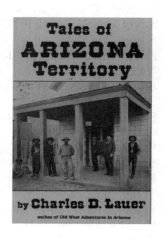

TALES OF ARIZONA TERRITORY

True stories of Arizona's pre-statehood history. Adventures and misadventures of pioneers, lawmen, desperadoes, stage coaches and stage stations.

5 1/2 x 8 1/2 — 160 Pages . . . $9.95

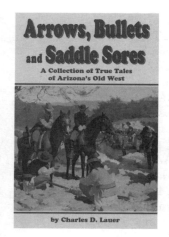

ARROWS, BULLETS and SADDLE SORES

True Tales of Arizona's Old West

Fascinating and true stories about events, places and people from Arizona's history. Read about the *Wickenburg Massacre, The Earps' Wives and Women, Gun Battle at Stockton Ranch, Battle of Apache Pass* and more! Includes maps and photos.

5 1/2 x 8 1/2—184 pages . . . $9.95

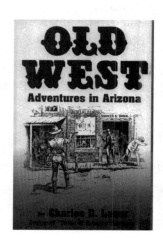

OLD WEST ADVENTURES IN ARIZONA

In the Arizona Territory men played for keeps! It was a place where the romance of stagecoach travel was interrupted by murder from ambush . . . where raiding was a way of life. The place names of Arizona's history still ring with vibrant memories of a glorious past.

5 1/2 x 8 1/2—176 pages . . . $6.95

ORDER BLANK

GOLDEN WEST PUBLISHERS

☼ 4113 N. Longview Ave. • Phoenix, AZ 85014

www.goldenwestpublishers.com • 1-800-658-5830 • FAX 602-279-6901

Qty	Title	Price	Amount
	Arizona Adventure—*Arizona Trilogy Vol. 1*	9.95	
	Arizona Cook Book	9.95	
	Arizona Legends & Lore	9.95	
	Arizona Trails & Tales	14.95	
	Arizoniana—*Arizona Trilogy Vol. 3*	9.95	
	Chili-Lovers' Cook Book	6.95	
	Cowboy Cartoon Cookbook	7.95	
	Cowboy Slang	6.95	
	Explore Arizona!	6.95	
	Ghost Towns in Arizona	12.95	
	Haunted Arizona: Ghosts of the Grand Canyon State	12.95	
	Haunted Highway: The Spirits of Route 66!	12.95	
	Hiking Arizona	6.95	
	In Old Arizona—*Arizona Trilogy Vol. 2*	9.95	
	Marshall Trimble's Official Arizona Trivia	8.95	
	Salsa Lovers Cook Book	6.95	
	Snakes and other Reptiles of the SW	9.95	
	Tales of Arizona Territory	9.95	
	Wild West Characters	6.95	

U.S. Shipping & Handling Add:	1-3 Books $5.00		
(Shipping to all other countries see website.)	4+ Books $7.00		
	Arizona residents add 8.1% sales tax		

Total $_____

(Payable in U.S. funds)

☐ My Check or Money Order Enclosed

☐ MasterCard ☐ VISA ☐ Discover ☐ American Express Verification code_____

Acct. No. _____ Exp. Date _____

Signature _____

Name _____ Phone _____

Address _____

City/State/Zip _____

Call for a FREE catalog of all our titles
— Prices subject to change —